Slightly Fractured

Memories

Dorothy,

Thanks for your cute story. It fit right in to this book.

Doug Bowen

Slightly Fractured

Memories

A Collection of Friends' Stories

Doug Bowen

Mill City Press

Mill City Press, Inc.
2301 Lucien Way #415
Maitland, FL 32751
407.339.4217
www.millcitypress.net

Paperback ISBN-13: 978-1-66285-234-3
Ebook ISBN-13: 978-1-66285-235-0

How this book came to be

I went to my 25th high school reunion and was surprised by how people's memories of the same teachers, classmates, and events differed. After some research, I learned that experts tell us that our memories are only partially factual. Surprisingly, memories are also partly fiction.

A few years later, a cousin told me a story which was very funny but a little hard to believe. So, I checked with some of the other people involved in that adventure, and they told the same basic story with some interesting differences.

That was the beginning of this book. I started asking friends, family, coworkers, and so on, to share any funny, surprising, or inspirational stories they were willing to share. I assured my contributors that I would protect everyone's identity by changing names and places.

Many of the stories I got were funny, but people also started sending me some touching, meaningful, and unusual experiences. Some were personal stories, and some were family legends. I have shared most of their stories although a few went a little too far.

I have chosen to repeat them just as they were related to me with some minor editing. Most of the personal stories I received used the pronoun 'I' to tell the story, so keep in mind that most of these stories are <u>not</u> my own personal experiences—*in other words, although I did contribute a few memories, the "I" in these stories is not me.*

Every one of these stories is based on someone's actual experience, but how much, and which parts of their memories are fictional, is a mystery even to the people who shared them!

Dedication

I am deeply indebted to all those who contributed their stories to this collection. Thanks to those who submitted funny stories that will make people laugh. Laughter is good for our physical and mental health, and we need more of it in our lives. Those stories that inspire us to strive to be better people are also very much appreciated. Some contributors shared touching stories which help the readers to remember that we can overcome problems in life as others have done. I'm grateful for the stories that educate by showing us different places, peoples, and ways of thinking. Contributors of the more unusual stories challenge accepted ways of thinking about life in general. Finally, familiar stories about animals, families, and school friends remind readers of their own best memories, and the many times we have all had to learn how to approach life with more compassion and positivity.

My thanks also go out to all the friends who were generous in their feedback, suggestions, and editing of the various forms of this book as it came together.

By previous agreement, contributors' names will not be revealed. Any profit from the sale of this book will be distributed to a variety of charities.

Animal Anecdotes

Unexpected Events

Family Frolics

School Daze

Life's Lessons

New Places, New Friends

Unusual or Weird

Military Memories

Animal Anecdotes

Our lives would not be as comfortable or
interesting without animals

The Pig Caper

Mel was in college in the late sixties and had grown his hair longer, as was the style in those days. He was visiting his grandfather and favorite uncle for a few days over the Thanksgiving holiday.

One of his cousins was visiting from Hawaii, where she had met and married a local guy from the islands. This new in-law had convinced the family to forgo the traditional Thanksgiving turkey in favor of a luau complete with a traditional Hawaiian pig roast. He had already dug a fire pit in the front yard.

Mel had been taking quite a bit of ribbing about his long hair and the fact that he was driving a 'hippie' van with a bed and curtains and a loud eight-track stereo. So, when his favorite uncle asked him if he would go over to a neighbor's farm to pick up the pig, he said "Of course."

They found some plastic to put down in the back of the van to cover the floor because he didn't want the carcass to bleed on his shag carpeting. When he got to the farm, he was shocked to find that the pig was not butchered but alive! The farmer kept assuring him that the pig would just sit quietly on the floor while he drove it back to the home place.

However, the pig resisted mightily when they tried to get it in the van, and in the process of pushing the pig inside, it managed to pull the plastic off the carpeting. After getting in the pig in the van, it did indeed sit down and quietly look around, just as the farmer had predicted.

Mel had no choice but to start driving back to the home place. As soon as the car started to move, the pig went crazy. He jumped up on the bed in the back and proceeded to crap all over everything.

He jumped around and tried to get out by beating his head against the rear window. When that didn't work, he turned toward the front of the van, dropping little 'presents' with every move.

The pig then stuck his head up between the two front seats and tried to bite Mel. Mel was elbowing him with all his force to make him move back. When the pig did finally move back, Mel focused on driving down the country road as fast as he could.

Suddenly, the pig leaped up into the passenger seat. He banged his head against the side window for a few moments and then turned his attention on Mel. After a quick look, the pig launched himself at the driver's side window and ended up in Mel's lap.

Mel was trying to drive and at the same time fight off a squealing, kicking, hysterical animal that weighed over a hundred pounds. He was swerving back and forth across the road like a drunk man at 60 miles an hour.

Just when Mel thought he was getting the upper hand and pushing the pig off him, the pig accidentally kicked the transmission into reverse! All four tires squealed as the pig was immediately slammed against the windshield, which cracked on impact. The pig fell to the floor and lay there stunned.

Mel coasted into a local gas station and found that the pig must have knocked the transmission into neutral when he fell, so the van would actually still go when he put the transmission back in gear.

He shot off down the road to get the pig to the site of the luau before it woke up. When he got there, he asked quietly in a cold, steely voice, "Where and how do you want me to kill this damned animal?"

The group that had set him up had gathered to laugh and poke fun at his trials, but they immediately perceived that they had gone too far. They gathered around him and told him "Go clean up and relax and have a beer." They would take care of the rest.

That pig turned out to be quite delicious, and Mel gained a measure of respect from all who were there. However, the van was never the same. Even after a lot of cleaning, both personal and professional, it seemed to Mel that it still smelled of pig even though no one else could smell it.

A Trip on the Amazon

In December of 2018, I led a group of five teenagers on a trip in the Amazon Rainforest in Brazil. After arriving, our guide Gabe, who speaks good English, his wife, and their daughter, picked us up. Gabe is an indigenous Indian, and his wife is a mix of several races which is typical in Brazil. Like all Brazilians, the family was always in a good mood, laughing and smiling.

A boat took us out into the Amazon River to the "Meeting of the Waters", where the black waters of the Rio Negro meet the sandy beige-brown waters of the Rio Solimoes. We could see the boundary between the two colors of water for miles! The Amazon is about two miles across at this place when not flooding.

We crossed over to the other side, and after a bumpy trip on a dirt road, we got into an old, ten-seater motor-canoe guided by an ancient Indian. He seemed to derive great pleasure in pointing out the alligators waiting on the riverbanks. In Portuguese he said, "They are just waiting for the boat to capsize, and they are looking forward to a good meal!"

However, the kids were not easily intimidated, and soon the old Indian was content to show us the amazing wildlife along the river without trying to scare us.

After two hours, we arrived at Gabe's large island. It had been in his family's possession for many years. He had been able to safeguard it from the land robbers who have been stealing land from the indigenous people for many years. Unlike many Indians, he had ancient documents proving long-standing ownership. His parents lived on this island all year.

There was a rickety landing on the island, and up on a little hill were five wooden cabins. There was also a large cabin with a dining room, as well as a kitchen and storeroom in back. For the next four days, we would eat exclusively what we ourselves caught in the river, or what grew in the huge vegetable garden, and eggs (as well as a few of the chickens.)

Later that evening, we all went out in the big canoe. There is no light pollution whatever, and the sky is wondrous to behold with its sea of stars, and the Milky Way like a silvery band across it.

Gabe shone a strong flashlight at the edge of the water. Right away we saw an incredible number of eyes dazzled by the light–alligators! The light immobilized them, making it easy for Gabe to grab a three-foot fellow. He held it tightly by its throat and just above the tail.

Gabe showed us what to do, and we all took turns holding a small alligator in our very own hands!

After breakfast the next day we went on a trek through the dense jungle. Gabe was an endless source of information. He knew every plant, tree, bird, snake, and insect, and he could make sounds that attracted monkeys.

After lunch we boarded the canoe and went fishing in some very still side waters of the big river. We were fishing for black piranhas. These are about a foot long and quite edible. They turned out to be delicious, together with rice grown right on their island.

There was no electricity on the island, so Gabe's family lit oil lamps next to each cabin. Sleep back at the camp was frequently interrupted by howling, screeching, and weird noises from the jungle all around us. I woke up about two in the morning because I heard some strange noises. Looking through a crack next to my bed, I saw a spotted creature moving silently under the cabin. Then we heard Gabe's voice saying calmly, but loudly, "Don't anybody go outside, there is a jaguar moving through the camp. Then he hit a gong or bell, and the jaguar took off. Needless to say, none of us went outside the rest of the night.

The next morning, we took to the canoe again and rode along the riverbank, a canopy of huge trees over us. Gabe pointed out monkeys, sloths, birds, and the alligators.

Suddenly one of the students said, "There is an animal floating in the water!" Gabe quickly turned the canoe around, and when we approached the woolly bundle floating in the water, he said to grab it quickly. His daughter scooped it out of the water, just five feet from the closest alligator. It turned out to be a little sloth.

We all held it in turn. It was soaking wet, but its smiling face told us that it knew that it was safe. Gabe told us that sloths were good swimmers, but this one most likely had fallen off an overhanging branch and would have been history without our spotting it.

He said there were many trees on his family's island with the kind of leaves the sloths preferred. We could take it to a safe place on his private island.

We were all in a kind of jubilant mood and couldn't stop taking pictures of "Klutzy," our little rescued sloth. We watched it as it climbed up its new tree on the island, at a very slow speed—about two feet every three hours. I wonder if somewhere in its little, furry head, it remembers the American tourists who saved its life!

It definitely was the trip of a lifetime!

Rotten Apples

One day Grandma sent my sister and me to help Grandpa pick some apples. There was one big, old apple tree right in the middle of the furthest pasture. We took the horses and wagon because Grandma said we would have to be higher up to reach the apples.

Grandpa decided that he also needed to bring a couple of the cows in that pasture back to the barn when we finished picking apples.

When we got over there, my sister and I were surprised to see all the cows around the tree. I asked Grandpa, "Are they trying to find some shade?" as it was a hot day.

He laughed and said, "No, they like apples, too." Us kids were surprised, and my sister said, "But Grandpa, they can't pick them. The apples are too high."

By then we were getting close enough to notice there were lots of rotten apples on the ground. We were squishing some of them under the wheels of the wagon. Grandpa said, "When apples get too ripe, they fall off."

Most of the cows had moved a short distance away. He stopped the wagon under a branch with lots of apples on it and set up the ladder in the back of the wagon. It was our job to climb up and hand the apples down to him. When we ran out of apples that we could reach, he would move the wagon to a different branch.

We filled up two bushel baskets with apples. I was surprised when Grandpa told me to drive the wagon back the way we came. Grandpa was walking among the cows and started herding a couple of them after us.

When we got to the gate, Grandpa told me to stop. He opened the gate, and when the cows passed us, he got back in the wagon, and I closed the gate. We slowly moved out the gate and onto the dirt road back to the house. He kept the cows walking ahead of us, using his whip to make cracking noises. He would never hit them.

My sister noticed it first as I was daydreaming about being allowed to drive the horses for the first time. She asked Grandpa, "Is something wrong with those cows?"

I came out of my daze and noticed that the rear end of one of the cows had sort of swung out to her side, and she was almost walking sideways. Then a few steps further, she fell into the ditch!

Grandpa got down from the wagon and coaxed her up and out of the ditch. She just stood there shaking her head like she didn't know what had happened.

Then the other cow got frightened of a small yellow butterfly. She mooed loudly and tried to turn around to run. But she was uncoordinated and each time she tried to turn, she went too far and ended up headed the same way back towards the butterfly. Grandpa grabbed her on one of her spins and slapped her on the rump so that she would go on down the road.

Finally, we were back on the wagon headed home. Grandpa then explained that the cows were drunk. When the ripe apples fell off the tree and lay in the hot sun, they rotted and fermented and created alcohol.

When we got back to the house and brought our apples in to Grandma, my sister bragged to her that we had brought home two drunk cows, too.

Grandma looked at Grandpa and then they both burst out laughing.

Who Chose Who?

Usually, we choose our pets, but sometimes they choose us. I had gone to visit one of my distant cousins, and when they answered the door instead of "Hello," they said, "Do you want a dog?" It really took me by surprise as I had been thinking about getting a second dog to keep the pug I already had company since I was not home almost all day every day.

They led me through the house to the back yard where their three dogs stayed. They had a German Shepard, a Golden Retriever, and a small, nasty tempered, black Dachshund who ruled the roost.

They had found a dog wandering around the neighborhood a month earlier. They had put up signs and even paid for an ad in the paper to try to find the owners, but no one ever replied. He was a small, long-haired dog of mixed breed.

At first, we couldn›t find him as he was trying to stay away from the big dogs and as far away as possible from the yappy dachshund. He was under some shrubbery. I walked toward him thinking that he was too small to be a good companion for my pug.

I talked softly and calmly to him as I crossed the backyard. I stopped when I got about 5 feet from him and waited for some sign from him that I could come closer. I knelt down and said, "So, do you want to come live at my house?" He launched himself at my chest immediately. He snuggled down in my arms and looked at me with grateful eyes. He sat on my lap for the rest of the visit with the relatives, and so I took him home.

I had decided that I had to get him out of that small back yard with those big dogs. A friend of mine had recently lost her two small dogs, and I thought that maybe she would want to adopt this dog.

He needed a bath badly, but he didn't seem to relish the idea. He growled at me once, and I told him that if he didn't have a bath, he would have to stay out in the garage. He seemed to understand because he submitted to the rest of the bath without resisting.

After the bath, I realized that he must have some Pomeranian blood because his coat was that particular brilliant reddish brown that I had only seen on that breed. He was such an intelligent animal that I soon found myself talking to him like a person.

I called my friend, but she declined my offer as it was too soon after her loss to think about another dog. I was stuck with him, but I didn't really mind as he was very sweet and happy. I named him Huli which is Chinese for fox because he looked like a fox and was so smart.

I was right about his size. Miji, my pug, walked right over him and pretended that he didn't even exist. Pugs are human centered after all, but the presence of another dog, whether acknowledged or not, did seem to calm Miji down. One good thing about Miji's lack of awareness of Huli was that Miji never seemed to be jealous when Huli sat in my lap. To Miji's way of thinking, as long as it wasn't food I had in my arms, he didn't care.

After a few years, I noticed that Miji started interacting with Huli. From then on they were inseparable. Huli was the smart one and he taught Miji many things. Probably the most important was how to use smell to find things. Miji's short nose was not very useful to him most of the time, but he learned by watching how to sniff things out. He often looked like he was trying to stand on his head as he buried his very short nose deep in the grass.

Huli and I became very close. A few years ago, I went to Europe for six weeks. I had a homestay student living with me at the time, and he had agreed to care for the dogs while I was gone. By then, the vet thought that Huli was probably almost 20 years old. He had almost no teeth and had cataracts, too.

I told the student that if Huli died while I was gone, he should bury him in the rose garden which was one of his favorite places. The student got very upset and said that he didn't want to take care of the dogs if Huli was going to die. I told him that I had no control over that, and just told him that because I didn't want him to feel responsible if it happened.

My student had observed our special relationship and so he asked me to tell Huli not to die while I was gone. I felt a little silly, but Huli and I did talk about it.

Huli was still going when I got back six weeks later, but he was not in good shape. He could only eat soft things that were hand fed to him. His back legs shook so bad at times that he couldn't walk. He found it hard to find his way outside and down the ramp into the back yard.

I took him in my arms and thanked him for waiting. I also told him that I didn't want to have to make the decision to end his life, and that he had my blessing if he was ready to go. I held him or kept him near me all day, and that night he left this world. I buried him in the rose garden like I promised.

I still miss that special dog that chose me.

He Gave Us the Bird!

My husband was one of those old-time doctors who made house calls. One of his patients was an older, house-bound gentleman named Mr. Jones. He lived next door to us, so it was easy for my husband to check on him.

Some friends had given Mr. Jones a mynah bird and told him that he could teach it to talk. He spent a lot of time with the bird and, since my husband came by often, the bird learned to say, "What's up Doc" and "Call me in the morning."

The first time the mynah bird talked in front of my husband, he was quite surprised. Mr. Jones laughed at the look on his face. My husband was always surprised because the bird sounded exactly like Mr. Jones' voice.

When the old man died, we were surprised to find out that he had left his bird to us. With three school-aged kids around, that bird learned to say many new things in his time with us.

That bird was quite curious and intelligent. He learned how to open the door of his cage. We tried different mechanisms for the latch, but he always figured them out and released himself.

Unfortunately, one day one of the kids didn't close the back screen door firmly and a neighbor's cat got in. We guessed that he had never seen a cat before, or he would have flown to safety, but the cat got him, and that was his undignified end.

We had a little service for the kids to grieve his passing, and in our minds, we all heard him say "Goodbye" in Mr. Jones' voice, as he had so many times before, when we were going out the door.

Beauty and the Beast

I have a friend who works as a representative for a big national company. As part of her job, she constantly travels all over the country.

One day after her meetings, she decided that she wanted to take her rental car up into the nearby mountains to enjoy the spectacular scenery. As she came around a curve, a small animal darted out of the brush onto the road, and she hit it. She thought it was a dog, but when she got out to look, she found that it was a small bear cub. It was breathing, but not moving.

She got out her cell phone and called a new friend she had met at the meeting earlier. As she described the situation, he started screaming, "Get back in the car! Get back in the car, NOW!" over and over again. She thought he was being a little hysterical, but she got back in her rental car and locked the doors.

When she looked up, she saw the big momma bear was hurtling down the road straight at her car. The bear leaped on the hood, slid across it, and hit the windshield full force. It shattered. The mama bear seemed woozy, but she started to claw at the broken windshield.

She realized that she had to get out of there, so she started the car and turned around in the middle of the road, knocking the dazed mama bear off as she peeled off down the road.

At the base of the mountain, there were two police cars waiting. Her friend had called the police and explained what he knew about the situation from the phone call.

She broke down shaking and crying and became incoherent. She finally settled down after some hot coffee, and as she was thanking the police, another official truck pulled up. It was the game warden He told her that he had checked, and the bear cub had died, so he would have to give her a ticket for killing a protected animal.

Just then her friend arrived and told her to repeat the story she had told him slowly and carefully. When she finished, the warden said, "Well, if the cub ran out in front of you, that's a different story." He let her go back to her motel room.

The next morning, she called her office and told them that she needed to take some time off immediately. When the office finally got the whole story, they began referring to the incident as "The Beauty and the Beast."

The Farmer's Wife

Anyone who has spent any time around cows knows that they are usually quite docile animals. They spend their days walking around eating and don't much care about the human beings around them, but sometimes they surprise you.

A cousin of mine sold a cow to a neighbor a few miles away. He decided that the easiest way to get her there was to load the cow into his pickup truck, so he put the four-foot-high cattle guards on the sides of the truck. Then he tried to get her to walk up a ramp into the truck.

The cow didn't want to go in the truck even with a lot of pushing from behind. He went to the barn and got a length of rope and tied it around her neck. He fed the rope through the slats in the cattle guards and gave the end to one of his sons.

Then, with one son pulling and the other son pushing, they tried again. They almost got her in, but at the last minute that cow surprised them and jumped to the side.

He went back to the barn and found an old electric cattle prod. He tested it, but of course, the batteries were dead. He called the boys over and told them to go get some batteries out of their many electronic toys for the prod.

All this time, old Bossy was getting more and more upset, and wanted to go back to the barn. When the boys finally found enough batteries, the battle started again, with one son pulling and the old man and the other son pushing. At the right moment, dad told the son to zap the cow in the butt with the electric prod.

But since her tail was flapping back and forth in frustration, that was not as easy as it sounded. Finally, the boy made a jab at her and caught her right in her most private and sensitive parts.

Not only did that cow go up into the truck, but she also actually jumped over the four-foot cattle guard! As she came down on the other side, her weight pulled the other son up in the air. He was now sitting on the cab of the truck, and the cow was choking on the other side.

The old man told the boy to let go of the rope, and as the boy landed on his side of the truck, the cow took off running on the other side. The boys looked at their dad who was just standing there shaking his head.

Just then their mom called from the house, "Come on in here. I just took an apple pie out of the oven." Without a word, they all turned and shuffled towards the house.

As they sat around the table eating fresh warm pie with ice cream, there was no conversation. They all just focused on the food in front of them.

Ten minutes later, their mom collected their plates and said, "You boys had better get that cow over to the neighbor." The boys looked at her incredulously.

"We had a little trouble getting her loaded," the old man said in an understated way, which made the boys laugh.

"Yeah, I know," mom said with a twinkle in her eye, "But she's ready to go now."

They got up and went to the window, and there was that cow standing in the back of the truck chewing on some hay. The boys cheered, and they all went out, closed up the truck bed, and took the cow to her new home.

On the way back, one of the boys wondered, "How come she came back and went right in the truck?"

"Well, how come we all went in the house when she ran away?" asked Dad.

"Well, 'cause mom had pie for us," the younger son replied.

"Yep, your mom knows what makes all critters move, and she was smart enough to put some of that cow's favorite alfalfa hay in the front of the truck bed. She knew that's always been old Bossy's favorite."

Cats and Dogs

When our daughter was four years old, my wife took her to see her grandparents in another state. About a week after they left, I read an article in a magazine detailing the importance for young children to grow up with pets.

As luck would have it, that same afternoon I drove past a farm where there was a sign saying, "Labrador/Sheltie Puppies–Free." I drove in, and there were five of them! As I walked up to the fence, the smallest of the puppies came waddling toward me.

The farmer came out and asked which one of the pups I wanted. I pointed to the little one, but the farmer said, "She is the runt of the litter. I don't think she will live long; pick another." But I took the little female pup as fate had directed me. As I drove home, she snuggled up to me, and I fell in love with her.

When I got home a surprise awaited me on our porch. Someone had dropped off a little black kitten with a white spot on his head. I put the puppy down on the porch, and those two fell in love.

That afternoon I called my wife. I was a bit apprehensive to tell her about the two little creatures, but to my surprise she said that she had been thinking about getting a pet for our daughter for some time. We decided to let our daughter choose the names for our two new animals. Apparently, she spent the next week thinking about names and drawing hundreds of pictures of dogs and cats.

I took both animals to the vet for the necessary shots. My wife told me that our daughter had decided on the names "Pepper" for the male kitten, and "Pepita" for the female puppy. I started calling them by their new names right away to get them used to the sound. They were inseparable from the start, and they felt an instant connection to our daughter when she and my wife came home.

The years went by, and Pepita and Pepper shared the same blanket, ran around the yard together, chased butterflies and frogs, rolled around in the snow in winter, and insisted on sharing the back seat of the car with our daughter whenever we went places.

Both had collars with their names, our names, and phone numbers just in case they ever got lost. As Pepita became older, she took to hopping on the golf carts at the golf green near our house. She often stayed with the golfers for most of the afternoon.

Every golfer knew her and carried snacks for her. When there were two or three carts near our place, they competed for Pepita's favors. It became a badge of good luck if Pepita chose your cart for the afternoon.

Pepper and Pepita preferred spending their nights under a comfortable bush outside near the front door, except during winter or rainstorms. Sixteen happy years passed, and Pepita began slowing down, but her love for us and Pepper was unshaken.

One morning when I called for her, only Pepper came out from under the bush. He was meowing like he never had before. Pepita had passed away peacefully in her sleep. We all cried and cried. There had never been a little dog more loving and sweet!

Pepper knew instinctively what had happened, and he yowled incessantly for a week. Then he became strangely silent.

My wife said, "Now Pepper will follow Pepita very soon because he can't live alone without his lifelong friend."

I answered, "But he still seems healthy!"

"Yes, in his body, but his heart is broken," explained my sensitive wife.

My wife was right. The next day, I found Pepper under the bush he had shared with Pepita for so many years.

His spirit had joined his most beloved companion.

A Lesson in Genetics

Grandpa and Grandma milked about eight cows every morning and evening for years. I was not allowed to go with them when they milked because they said I spooked the cows, but I spent time with the cows at other times, and helped feed them in the winter, when they stayed in the barn most of the time.

In the summer, they got to go out in the pasture after the morning milking. Every year some of the cows stopped giving milk.

One of the cows that came into heat (ready to breed) the summer when I was ten, was a small, beautiful Brown Swiss. She was my favorite because she was so gentle, and she was a great milker. One of Grandpa's neighbors wanted to breed that particular cow with his bull.

This cow was also the oldest of Grandpa's milk cows, so he wasn't sure if it would work out. Since the neighbor lived just a mile away, I was supposed to walk her over there. I was proud that Grandpa trusted me to do that.

I was strolling along the road leading that cow, enjoying the breeze and the birdsong, when a loud snort sounded from somewhere behind me. I looked around and froze as there was a big, black and white Holstein bull in the road behind me. I had never seen him before, and I didn't know where he had come from.

He started toward me and I freaked out. I glanced around and saw a tree nearby. I started to run toward the tree, pulling the cow after me, but after a few steps, she stopped and wouldn't come any farther. The bull was coming faster now, so I dropped the rope, ran, and climbed the nearest tree.

Nature then took its course, and I got a lesson in anatomy and procreation. Apparently, the breeze had alerted any bull in the area that there was an available cow nearby.

The bull soon drifted off down the road, so I climbed down, grabbed the rope and took the cow the rest of the way to the neighbor's farm.

I didn't tell the neighbor or my grandfather what had happened because I was ashamed that I had run and hid in a tree. A week later the farmer brought the cow back and told Grandpa that she wasn't in heat after all, and his bull wasn't interested in her.

Later when she started showing signs of her pregnancy, Grandpa thought that maybe the neighbor had been wrong. Next spring, the little Brown Swiss cow delivered a female calf.

The calf was bigger than expected, and over the next couple of years, grew to be taller than the other cows and was just generally bigger all over.

She was also unusual in color. She was the only cow Grandpa had ever seen with three colors – black, white, and brown. Of course, I knew that big cow was the offspring of that small Brown Swiss cow and the big Holstein bull.

Grandpa put two and two together and asked me if I knew anything about what had happened. When I told him the truth, he laughed, and then patted me on the head and told me that I had not done anything wrong.

Grandma named that cow Bessie. She had inherited her father's size and her mother's ability to produce milk. Grandma always milked her. Most cows gave a bucket of milk each, but Bessie gave enough milk to fill up two buckets! Grandma always said that hers was the best tasting milk.

Grandpa and Grandma sold milk and eggs in town every week, but they kept Bessie's milk for themselves. We used it to make butter, and of course, to drink. Grandma always said that the cream from Bessie's milk made the best 'ram Schlag' which is German for whipped cream.

Later, when I studied genetics in college, I found that hybrids such as Bessie often outperform their parents. I began to wonder why people think that there is something special about a pure-bred animal. It seems to me one of the reasons Americans are so successful in so many areas is because most of us are hybrids.

To Bite or Not to Bite

I have led over forty student trips to Mexico, but two stand out for animal-related incidents.

The last point on this particular itinerary was a visit to the Ixta-Popo State Park near Mexico City. The Popocatepetl Volcano and its sister volcano Ixtaccihuatl are the names of the two volcanoes that give the park its name.

The names are based on a beautiful ancient legend about the love between the daughter of one chieftain and the son of another tribe's leader. Their tribes had been enemies forever, but one week every year they called a truce to trade goods.

These two young people fell in love. Their pleas for marriage were rejected by their fathers, so the two lovers eloped during the annual truce. They tried to hide in the mountains but were soon overtaken by cold and hunger.

The warrior built a fire to keep them warm. The princess fell asleep while the warrior tried to blow warmth from the fire over his love. Unfortunately, in the morning they were both found frozen to death.

The Gods looked down upon the scene and were touched by their love, so they created the two volcanoes–Ixtaccihuatl, "the Sleeping Woman," and Popocatepetl, "the Smoking Warrior"–to honor their forbidden love.

As travelers approach the volcanoes, they can clearly see the outlines of a female lying on her back–Ixtaccihuatl and the constant puffs of smoke issuing from the top of Popocatepetl.

My students and I had parked our vans on a street in the town at the foot of the two towering volcanoes. We were getting ready to hike up one of the paths to the Popo volcano.

I had just finished telling the story of the great love and sad fate of the sweethearts when suddenly a door across the street opened and a big dog came running out barking. He jumped at one of the girls and clamped his teeth right into her rear end. Then just as quickly as he had bitten her, he ran off.

I asked a passer-by for the nearest doctor's office. Luckily, his office was just around the corner. After sending the rest of the group to the market to shop, I took the girl there. When we entered, we found the waiting room full. I explained the situation to the crowd, and nobody objected when the doctor took us in right away.

After thoroughly cleaning the four puncture wounds and giving her two injections, the doctor instructed her to get two more injections after returning to the USA the next day. We left, and unbelievably, we didn't have to pay a single peso! "Cortesia de Mexico," the sweet old doctor said.

Just as we were leaving the office, a man came running in and asked if anyone had heard of a girl being bitten. I told him that she was part of my group, and the gentleman said that the dog was his, that he was so sorry. He insisted on treating our whole group to dinner to make up for his dog's misdeed. He would not take no for an answer.

Later that evening, after going up almost to the snow line on Popo, we all had a scrumptious dinner, courtesy of the dog's owner. The rest of the trip we talked a lot about the old doctor, the dog, and his owner, and why Mexico is so unforgettable!

On some of these trips, we would conclude our stay in Mexico with a five-day stay in Acapulco. For swimming, sun-bathing, and home-cooked Mexican food, we left the city, and drove south to where foreign tourists were rarely if ever seen.

The waters were warm, and the waves broke about 50 yards from the shore. My instructions to the kids were strict and succinct. Absolutely no going out beyond the visible breaking point of the waves. Always stay close to one another in twos or threes and keep an eye on possible signals from the beach.

I was sitting in a beach chair occasionally looking up from the book I was reading when I spotted something that l instantly knew was trouble. One of the boys was bobbing around about 300 yards offshore. I got up and walked to the water's edge, where several of my students joined me in yelling and waving at the guy to come back in.

At that very moment one of the Mexican lifeguards was running by with a fifteen-foot pole that had a red flag on top. He was yelling as he ran along the beach, "Tiburon! Tiburon!" which is shark in Spanish.

Needless to say, my heart stood still! The boy out in the Pacific didn't react at all, and soon there must have been a hundred people waving, yelling, and screaming at the top of their lungs.

I have since re-lived that moment many times and the absolute certainty that we were going to lose that boy. Finally, a small launch took off from the life-guard station, skipping over the waves to get the boy on board. They brought him to us, and he finally realized what might have happened to him for not listening and obeying my instructions.

I decided that it was necessary to set an example, so that evening I called the parents of the boy, and the very next morning I took the boy to the airport and sent him home, even though we had only a few days left in Mexico.

After talking to the young man's father on the phone, I was afraid that his dad's reaction was going to be scarier for him than the shark-bite that never happened.

Powder Puff Kitten

When I was a mailman walking routes all over a rather large town, I found a tiny kitten that barely had its eyes open. I looked around for the mother, but there were no cats in the area. I picked the kitten up and carried it in my mail pouch around my whole route. At every house where someone was home, I asked if the kitten was theirs, or if they knew whose it might be, but no one could help.

I ended up taking the kitten home. I went over to my sister's house and asked her what to do. She got out a very small baby bottle that was part of one of her daughter's play sets. We filled it with milk and the little kitten drank it greedily. My sister's daughter thought the fluffy kitten looked like her grandma's powder puff, so we named it Puff.

I took the tiny bottle home and fed the kitten as often as I could given my work schedule. I asked the cat lady next door to help with the feedings in the beginning when the kitten was small. That kitten grew like a weed, and soon it was obvious that it was a male. Puff seemed a completely inappropriate name but knowing that my niece would be disappointed if I changed it, I decided the cat wouldn't care.

I learned that mother cats teach their offspring how to care for themselves. Puff never learned to lick himself clean, so I had to bathe him. He didn't like it and yowled so loudly that the cat lady next door asked me what I was doing to make him protest so loudly. However, even though he made a fuss when I got him all wet, he never tried to bite or scratch me.

In the house with me, he was the sweetest, most affectionate cat I've ever known, but outside he was a tough, territorial monster. The only cats he would accept in our area were the cat lady's three cats next door. I never knew when I got home from work what shape he might be in. I spent quite a bit of money on visits to the veterinarian. In fact, when we came in the door, the vet often asked, "What now?"

He was a smart cat, too. He could tell from the tone of my voice how to respond. If someone I didn't know came to the door, and I had a negative tone, he would come to the door yowling and hissing aggressively. If a friend showed up, he would rub against their legs to show his acceptance.

Eventually, I had to move to another state, and I worried about taking him with me as he was so territorial. The neighbor lady solved the problem for me. She had recently lost one of her cats and said that since she had been feeding him off and on for years, she would take him in.

It was several years before I went back to the neighborhood to visit the cat lady. She was gone and the cats, too. I asked another neighbor where she had gone, and as I feared, I was told she had died. That neighbor told me that the a big yellow cat had stayed around the neighborhood for several years before he had finally disappeared.

I still think about that tough, sweet cat, and how silly I often felt when I went out onto the front porch and yelled "Puff, come in; it's time for dinner."

The Pony That Knew the Way Home

My great grandmother Trudy was born in 1880. When the blizzard of 1888 hit, she was eight years old and in third grade in a one-room country school a mile from her family's homestead farm. She told me this story when I was about ten years old.

The weather in January had been like a roller coaster. First, there had been deep snow, then the weather turned brutally cold, and then the weather cleared and warmed up. It almost seemed like spring.

January 11th was another warm day. Little Trudy went outside to use the toilet after lunch, and she noticed huge, black clouds off in the west. They reminded her of clouds in the summer just before a rainstorm. She told the teacher what she had seen when she went back in.

By 3:00 p.m. the sky had darkened, and a cold wind came up, rattling the windows in the schoolhouse. The teacher went out to see what was happening, and hurried back in. She was shocked by what she had seen—a wall of white moving toward them.

The students were staring out the windows at the snow, which had just started to fall. They could see that the horses that some students rode to school were moving nervously in their pen.

Within a few minutes the snow was so thick they couldn't see anything outside the window. The teacher decided to send the students home immediately. She started getting everyone ready to leave. She was surprised that some of the older boys had come to school that day without their heavy coats as it had started off as a warm day.

The teacher realized that the temperature was dropping fast. Ice was already forming on the inside of the windows. Later, they found out that the temperature dropped more than 60 degrees and it was below zero in a matter of minutes. She tried to organize the students who had walked to school to walk beside someone on a horse that was going in the same general direction.

Trudy's pony was named Cookie. She loved her and rode her to school every day. Six other children lived in the direction she was going so they were told to stay together along the way. By the time they were all ready to go, the snow was so thick and the wind so fierce that they couldn't even see each other. They had to hold hands to stay together.

Trudy talked to her pony and told her to go home. She knew that the pony knew the way home as she had made that same trip after school for several years. She grabbed the pony's tail in one hand and a classmate's hand in the other and they all started toward home.

It was slow going and some of the kids kept slipping and falling as the road got icy and hands and feet got numb, but after about forty-five minutes, the pony stopped. Trudy led the school kids along the side of the pony and into her family's barn. Her school mates huddled in the hay out of the wind while Trudy felt her way along the fence to find her way to the house.

Her mother and father came out and brought all the children into the house to warm up. Little did they know at the time that they would be stranded together there for the next two days while the storm blew itself out. The whole world had become a great white desert.

Her father had to climb out of the attic window to scoop out the front door of the house and to get to the barn to check on the animals. He didn't tell Trudy right away that her pony Cookie had frozen to death. The pony was encased in a thick coat of icy snow, and even inside the barn, it wouldn't melt due to the below zero temperatures.

Eventually, when people were able to get out and around, it was discovered that a number of school children had frozen to death trying to get home. Some adults who were at work and had decided to try to find their children and families, also perished in the blizzard.

Some of the schoolchildren's parents had gone out looking for their kids and suffered frostbite. People lost fingers, toes, ears, noses, or even lower legs due to the extreme cold. The parents of the children that had come home with Trudy were elated and rapturous when they found out that their kids who they believed had been victims of the storm, had survived after all.

Great-Grandma always said that her pony Cookie saved her life and the lives of her schoolmates that fateful day. She never wanted another pony or rode another horse in her life after that fateful storm.

A number of livestock also died in the storm which by then was known as the 'Schoolhouse Blizzard.' Just a few weeks later, a similar storm hit the East Coast of the U.S., also killing a number of people and animals.

That East Coast storm was called 'The Great Blizzard,' but the people in the Midwest thought that the 'Schoolhouse Blizzard' had been just as bad.

Unexpected Changes

Life has a way of surprising us in ways we
didn't see coming

First Impressions

One day at lunch, I asked a group of friends if anyone knew about dyslexia. Of course, some of them knew about the condition in which people see shapes and words differently than others. Then I asked them if they knew of a similar condition that meant someone who hears things differently from the way most people do.

After my friends had a good laugh, I went on to explain that I was one of those people who heard things differently, and that it gets me into trouble every so often. My husband even had me take a hearing test, but the doctor said that I had no hearing problems.

For instance, I was working for a big company as a trainer for their software products. On one occasion, I was in Atlanta training a group on a new piece of software. After I had gone through the PowerPoint presentation, I turned to the group and said, "Now, I know that all the diagrams and talk in the world are not worth five minutes of experience. So, has anyone downloaded the software onto their workstation yet?"

A gentleman in the back raised his hand. "Thank you, sir, and what is your name?" He replied with his southern drawl something which sounded like "aahm eyud" to me.

I spoke a little longer about the software and then I said,

"All right, let's all go over to Ahmed's workstation and see how this program really works."

The group shrieked with laughter because I thought the guy's name was Ahmed! All the while the guy in the back just scratched his head and kept repeating, "Ed, Ed," still making it sound like two syllables. I had heard something quite different from "I'm Ed!"

Another time I remember this happening was when my boss asked me to meet some important clients for a ski weekend. My boss was hoping that I would hit it off with the wife and co-owner to help make the negotiations go a little easier.

He warned me that the wife was a little difficult and that she usually made all the final decisions. As she and I were going up the ski lift together, I said, "This is going to be a fun weekend."

I heard the woman answer, "I doubt it. I have panda shoes."

Since it was quite cold and we both had covered the lower half of our faces with wool scarves, I recognized that I had probably heard wrong.

Several minutes passed while I tried to figure out what the woman actually said when I realized that the woman was staring at me.

The silence had gone on too long and was becoming uncomfortable. So, I chose a neutral statement and said, "Well, how do you feel about that?"

The woman looked at me scornfully and said, "Well, what do you think? and this cold weather isn't helping."

We soon arrived at the top of the lift, and as we got off, I decided to own up and said, "I may have misunderstood. Did you say that you have panda shoes?"

The woman looked shocked and disgusted and said, "I have hand issues," and quickly skied away. She didn't speak to me the rest of the day.

So much for first impressions! Somehow, we got the contract anyway.

Love's Lightning

I am fully aware that most, if not all, married couples have interesting stories to tell of how they met, and how they knew they were made for one another. I met my future wife in a rather crazy way.

I had just passed my 46th birthday, living a blissfully unmarried, irresponsible, and worry-free life in Rio de Janeiro, where I was teaching English. I had experienced a number of serious, and not-so-serious, relationships in my life. I had almost gotten engaged several times, but the prospect of a settled lifestyle made me wiggle out of any commitments. Some might call it cowardice, which would be correct.

On December 17, 1985, schools had just closed for the summer (summer in the southern hemisphere is exactly opposite the winter season in the USA). I was sitting on Copacabana Beach at about 1:00 p.m. I was reading a book about explorers when suddenly a shadow fell over my book.

I looked up, and lightning struck. I felt a strange tingling all over my body. An unbelievably pretty young lady had just walked by and sat down on a colorful blanket about ten feet from me. I stared like I had lost all of my senses. She politely ignored me. She then took out a paperback book and started reading. (Most people still read books in the 80s, because cell phones had not been invented yet.)

Then the game began. I felt the girl looking at me, and like a shy schoolboy, I whipped my book up in front of my face, and then I looked at her over the top of my book. She, in turn, covered her face with her book and looked back at me. This went on a number of times. I felt too shy to say anything for the first time in my life where a young lady was concerned. All I could think was, "This is the one. I was right to wait all these years!"

Yet I was too smitten to be able to even croak one syllable, even though my Portuguese was quite good. I kept peeking at her, and she kept glancing back at me. We played that silly game with the books in front of our faces for more than an hour, until finally this beautiful, unknown creature got up, gathered her belongings, shrugged, and walked off. I stayed where I was, absolutely paralyzed, and inwardly cursing my idiocy. When I finally collected my wits and got up, she had disappeared into the crowd on the beach.

Needless to say, I spent a tortured evening and night tossing and turning and fretting about how I had probably ruined my future with my cowardice. I went back to the same place the next day, and the day after that, and for several more days, but my sweet lady never showed up again.

I gave up and went to a beach out of town to stop torturing myself hoping that she would show up. I was sitting on the beach with a cold drink when a paper blew by and stuck to the moisture on my drink bottle. It was an advertisement for one of the biggest soccer games of the year. It was happening on that very day. I decided that I had to go. These games on Sunday always started at 6:00 p.m., and it was already 3 o'clock.

I hopped into my car and drove like a maniac back into Rio, making it into the vicinity of the stadium at about 5:00. When the world-famous Maracana stadium was built for the 1950 World Cup, very few people in Rio had cars, so no provisions were made for parking. Eventually, the growing city completely engulfed the stadium area. In desperation I drove through the streets, alleys, and lanes in the hills above the stadium looking for a place to park. Finally, I found an open spot. I backed my car into the space and was in the process of locking it when I heard a voice coming over a flowering hedge: "You can't park there. That is my dad's reserved space!" I looked up, and lightning struck me a second time – it was the girl from the beach!

Stuttering and stammering, I explained that I was going to the soccer game at the stadium. She answered, "No, don't go to the game, I would like you to meet my mother. Please come inside!"

I had been in Brazil long enough to know about Brazilian customs, so I understood that this was the way girls obtained permission from their parents to go out on a date. I went inside. The main room was full of sisters, brothers, and many children, and on a throne-like chair sat a stately, dignified lady who looked at me with a questioning face.

Then the girl said, "Mom, this is the man I saw on the beach. He didn't have the courage to open his mouth!" The whole room had suddenly fallen silent, and everyone was looking at me. Her mother asked, "Sir, what do you want from my daughter?"

Then lightning struck for a third time, because I surprised myself when I said, "Ma'am, I wish to marry her!"

Her mother extended both arms upward, smiled, and said, "God has answered my prayers!" Everybody cheered like only Brazilians can. Then the oldest brother asked the girl, "Well, you heard him, what do you think?"

She replied, "I will take him, as soon as he tells me his name!"

I told her my name, and she told me hers. We were married exactly three weeks later. Nine months later, we had a beautiful daughter. All this happened 35 years ago, and I have never ever regretted having been struck by love's lightning!

The Technology Shuffle

"Time flies," is certainly true. I've had to confront all the changes that have come with time passing in many ways, but technology to me used to be a TV remote, a push-button phone, or a built-in oven timer.

In 1998, my daughter decided I needed a computer. "Everyone has one nowadays," she said. So, she brought her old computer over, showed me a few things it could do, and then just left!

For the next five years, I fiddled around with that computer and eventually learned how to use email, Map Quest and, best of all, I found all the online food channels for recipes.

Then a few years later, a friend visiting me said that my computer was too old and brought me a new one. So, the learning started all over again. I couldn't make it work the same as the old one. I thought I was doing something wrong.

Then one day my daughter showed up with a big box and said, "Here's a cappuccino machine that my husband bought, but now he doesn't want us to drink coffee for health reasons, so I thought you'd like it."

What had she been thinking? That thing looked like a robot from a science fiction movie! I had a friend take the box out to the garage after I found out there were no instructions in the box. I thought maybe my fourteen-year-old grandson could figure it out when he visited.

Next, my daughter gave me her 'old' digital camera. She had bought a newer, smaller one. The one she gave me is an expensive camera and I'm sure it takes great pictures, but after four years, I had just found out that my older camera, which I liked very much, had a switch to make it take videos as well as still pictures. How far behind am I?

My son sent me a DVD of my granddaughter's wedding, which I was unable to attend. He said, "Just pop it in your DVD player and enjoy!" At that point, I had just started to learn how to use my VHS cassette player, but I went out and bought a DVD player. After juggling three different remotes for more than an hour, I jumped for joy when the screen suddenly said DVD.

I watched the wedding video and pictures, and then tried to turn it off and get back to my regular TV programs. More than an hour later, I gave up and went to the kitchen to start dinner. When I came back into the living room, don't ask me how, but the regular TV was back on! I have finally learned how to use the DVD player because they don't make VHS cassettes anymore!

Now the world is into cell phones. My daughter got me one and even pays for it, no less; but every time she changes phones or companies, I get a new phone too. I'm on the third or fourth one now.

The newest one allows you to call without having to dial the number. You just say the name of who you want to call. Great, but sometimes it has trouble understanding me. I have learned that shouting at it does no good, so sometimes I just give up and find the number I need in my handy little personal phone book.

Will I ever catch up to all these changes in technology?

A Sudden Change of Style

The little girl with the golden curls was excited. Her name was Ellie Hays. She was sitting on the porch and looking down the road to town. She was waiting for her daddy. He had been gone for three whole days and she missed him.

The front door opened, and her mother came out to remind her that she had chores to do. Everyone on the farm had chores, no matter how old or young they were. She was five years old, so her job was to collect the eggs and feed the chickens, but she didn't want to do her chores today. After arguing with her mother, she grudgingly headed to the hen house.

As Ellie was coming out of the hen house, she caught sight of someone coming down the road. She ran towards the road, but quickly realized that the man wasn't her daddy.

Disappointed, she turned back towards the house with her egg basket. She had almost reached the door when she heard her daddy's voice calling her name. "Ellie, Ellie."

Her mother came out of the house as Ellie turned around. "Silas, is that you?" Her mother sounded confused. Ellie looked all around but didn't see her daddy, just that stranger from the road coming up the driveway.

"Where's Daddy?" she asked, almost ready to cry.

"I'm right here, Angel," said her father's familiar voice, but the voice was coming out of that strange man.

"Silas!" exclaimed her mother. "You sure do look different." Ellie was confused. How did her mother know this strange man who had her father's voice?

"I'm right here. Don't you know me, Ellie?" the man asked as he bent down to talk to her.

As tears ran down her cheeks, she cried, "What did you do to my daddy?" Then she slapped his face and ran into the house.

It took several days before Ellie could accept that the man with the short hair and clean-shaven face was her daddy. Her father had always had long curly hair like hers that touched his shoulders, and a big scratchy beard that she loved to run her fingers through.

Her father and mother tried to explain that the new fashion for men in the 1890s was to have short hair and shave off their beards, but it was a long time before she was comfortable with her father's voice coming from this 'new' man with short hair and no beard.

Many years later at a family dinner in the 1970s, Ellie's granddaughter asked her innocently how she liked her great -grandson's new hairstyle.

His mother was counting on great grandma to disapprove of his long 'Beatle' hairstyle, but Ellie sighed and disappointed his mother when she didn't disapprove, but said instead, "It reminds me of my father. I like it!"

Then she told the story of her father's haircut and shave.

What Did She Say?

Since I retired, I have been taking a ukulele class at the senior center. We meet once a week, and there are usually around 30 people in the group. I have made a lot of friends as there is plenty of time for socializing as well as learning to play the ukulele.

Humans are creatures of habit, and it seems that we all tend to sit in the same place every week. One of the ladies that I sit beside has a few problems with her hearing on occasion. She likes to sit beside me because I am a loud person, and I enjoy her great sense of humor.

One day we were asked to wear our Aloha wear for a group picture. We lined up on the steps and smiled, but the person taking the picture just couldn't seem to get one that she liked.

It was a new camera and kept giving her strange messages, so she finally asked us to come back next week dressed up again, and she would have a better camera to take the pictures.

It was a little chaotic getting everyone down off the plat-form that we had used to make rows for the picture. My friend took that moment to ask me what the woman taking the pictures had said.

Not wanting to take time to explain it all at that moment, I just said, "New pictures next week."

She drew back looking shocked and said, "Nude pictures?"

I roared with laughter, and she realized that she had heard me wrong. Going along with the joke, she said, "Well then, I guess I'll wear only my plastic flower lei!"

Beachfront Exposure

During the first part of my military service, I was stationed in Southern California. Since I had grown up in the Midwest, I loved spending time on the beach. One of my platoon mates grew up near the beach and taught me many things about how to ride the waves and be safe in the surf.

Since Disneyland and the San Diego Zoo were quite famous in the Midwest, my wife and I had a steady stream of visitors from back home. One of my high school buddies came out for a visit with his sister. His sister was married to a Navy man aboard a submarine which was due to dock in San Diego at about the same time.

They got to our place a few days before her husband was due to be in port, so they wanted to go to see the beach. The weather was beautiful, but the surf was up a little due to a storm somewhere off the coast. I really didn't want to swim that day, but they insisted that they had to be able to say they had been in the Pacific Ocean when they got back home.

I patiently tried to explain that every seventh to tenth wave would be bigger than the others, so with the current conditions, we had to be kind of careful. I told them that if we saw a big wave coming, we should run toward it not away from it and then dive through the wave face rather than trying to stand against it. Most people underestimated the power of ocean waves.

For the first fifteen minutes, we had a great time. The bigger waves, when they came, were not too much bigger than the others. Then I noticed that my friend and his sister were turned toward the beach yelling and waving to encourage my wife to come and join us. I had told them that she was a little afraid of the ocean, and thought it was too cold.

She stood up, and they thought she was going to come in, but she was pointing and yelling. I knew before I turned around that there was a really big wave behind us. I yelled, "Run!" as loud as I could at my two friends. My buddy didn't even look back; he just started running toward the beach.

His sister, who was near me, turned and looked at me with a confused look. I grabbed her arm and drug her as fast as I could out toward the coming wave. Just as we got close, I yelled, "Dive!" and went through the glassy wave face.

Her wrist, which had been in my hand, was jerked away. I was tumbled along the sandy bottom and finally came up sputtering and wiping seawater out of my eyes.

The first thing I saw was my wife knee deep in seawater as the wave had gone all the way up the beach and had drenched all the sunbathers. Next, I saw my buddy standing in knee deep water looking out to the ocean. He had blood streaming down his face and one shoulder.

Then I heard the screaming. His sister was a hundred feet down the beach and bellowing at the top of her lungs. She was disoriented and looking for the rest of us. She was also topless! Somehow, she had lost the top of her two-piece bathing suit.

She finally recognized her brother and went running up the rapidly draining beach. Apparently, she was so concerned with his injuries that she still had not realized that she was topless. He was so shocked at seeing her half-naked that he couldn't speak.

At the same time, my wife ran up with a dripping towel and tried to wrap it around her. She jumped when the cold, wet towel touched her skin, but instead of covering herself, she proceeded to dab at her brother's wounds with the towel. Since it was drenched in salt water, the wet towel only made his injuries sting more.

I arrived about that time, concerned for everyone. There were many other people on the beach injured that day. My buddy immediately realized that his injuries were all minor scrapes, and that they were his own fault for running the wrong way when the big wave came. He laughed and said, "This is not the introduction to the ocean I had dreamed about!"

At about the same time, his sister came to her senses and realized that her swimsuit top was missing. She grabbed the towel which was cold and bloody and started to cry. In a split second, she slipped into a rage and started beating me with the wet towel.

According to her, it was all my fault. Her brother tried to talk some sense into her, but she was beyond logic. My wife noticed her bathing suit top had washed up on the beach and retrieved it, but she bellowed, "I never want to see the damn thing again."

We made it back to our place, and everyone got cleaned up and finally settled down. After a strong cocktail or two, we all started to feel more mellow. After a few more cocktails, humorous comments started to slip into the conversation.

Her brother complimented his sister on the perkiness that she had been able to maintain at her age. She laughingly said that the cold water helped in that regard.

I tried to lessen her embarrassment by saying topless bars were all the rage in California, and that maybe she could get a job out here. She just rolled her eyes and giggled. I'm sure that she never told anyone back home this story about her first adventure with the ocean.

Well, I was Almost Right

I was entertaining my neighbor one evening, and I had been talking about the awesome bread that my daughter and her husband bought back from their trip to Oregon. They had brought me some of that bread, and it was really special and delicious.

Just then, some friends called from the big grocery outlet asking if I needed them to pick up anything for me. They also asked me what the name of that bread was so they could pick up a loaf for themselves.

Well, I admit that I have been known to get words wrong. Somehow, they get all crossed up in my brain. All I remembered was that it was made by a guy who had learned to bake in prison. At first, I thought maybe it was something like 'Murder Bread,' but then out of my mouth came "Drop Dead Bread".

My friends asked one of the clerks there if the store carried that 'Drop Dead' brand. The clerk looked and looked and finally came back and said, "Sorry we can't find any bread by that name".

A week later my daughter came over, and I told her about trying to find that awesome bread that they had been raving about.

She said, "You mean Dave's Killer Bread"? She saw the look on my face and said, "Mom, what did you call it?" I had to tell her! Now, my family and some of my friends like my new improved name, 'Drop Dead Bread'.

The name of the bread had nothing to do with crime or prison; "Killer" is just slang for something really good like "That's a killer idea." Then I realized that for some of us oldsters, "drop dead" also meant really good, like 'drop dead gorgeous."

I told you my brain mixes things up, but I was almost right!

P.S. Dave's Killer Bread is rated almost at the top of the list of healthy, nutritious breads by Consumer Reports Magazine.

The Mosquito

I was staying with a friend at his parents' house. After dinner, his dad excused himself, saying that he was going to turn in early as he had an important doctor's appointment the next day in another city and would have to leave early. His wife went upstairs with him. My friend's bedroom was also upstairs, and he said he had to work on a paper for school, so I was left alone.

I took a shower, put on my pajamas, read for an hour, and then decided to turn in early myself. Since they had given me the house tour when I arrived, I knew that the bedroom I was staying in was directly below the folks' room. I heard them talking and moving around for a while, and then all was quiet.

I was almost asleep when I heard a mosquito near my ear. I hate mosquitoes and tried to swat it away. It kept coming back. I finally got up and turned on the light. That mosquito was hard to find, but I finally spotted it sitting on the wall high up in a corner of the room. I looked around the room for something to swat it with but didn't see anything at hand.

Then I remembered that I was right under the parent's bedroom, so I had to be careful not to make any noise to wake them. For a moment, I considered climbing up on the desk in that corner to get closer, but decided that either the mosquito would fly away, or the old desk might give away under my weight.

Finally, I looked down and saw the underwear I had taken off when I went to shower. I wadded it up in a tight ball and threw it at the mosquito. Now, I never played sports when I was young, but somehow, I hit the damn thing. The mosquito and my underwear fell down behind the computer on the desk.

I silently cheered, turned out the light and went back to bed. About 15 minutes later, a mosquito buzzed around my ear. I threw back the covers, jumped out of bed, recovered my underwear from behind the computer, and searched for the mosquito's body. It was not there, so I guessed the first strike had only stunned it.

Now I was really mad. If it had been another mosquito, I would have thought the problem was bigger than I had first thought, but to be bugged by the same creature again was just too much. I had to search very carefully, but I finally found it resting on the wall above the bed.

I moved toward the mosquito at a very slow pace. Someone watching might have wondered if I was moving at all. I wanted to get close enough so that I wouldn't miss this time. When I was quite close, I stretched the elastic in the waistband out and snapped the mosquito on the wall. This time I found the body in the blankets and crushed it with one of my shoes.

I went back to bed with a smile on my face which then became an uncontrollable laugh which I had to suppress or wake up the folks upstairs. I held my breath, my ears popped, my eyes watered, and I covered my head with the blanket until I was able to gain a little control. Finally, welcome sleep came–uninterrupted by any mosquitoes.

A Mixed Blessing

I made an appointment to see my eye doctor as I was having some trouble reading and driving at night. I was not too surprised when he said I had cataracts as I have many friends my age who have already dealt with the same problem.

He made me an appointment for the surgery, reassuring me that it is relatively easy and painless. My daughter drove over to take me to and from the operation. I came home with a patch on my eye. I assured my daughter that I would be all right and she went home.

The next day, I could not believe how well I could see. I marveled at the view outside my windows. I had always enjoyed the scenery, but now everything seemed greener and more colorful and vibrant than before.

The doctor had told me to take it easy for a few days, so I was just relaxing in my recliner when I happened to look up at my ribbed vaulted ceiling and spotted a cobweb. On closer inspection, I saw a number of cobwebs.

I was horrified as I had always considered myself the kind of woman who kept a spotlessly clean house. I considered trying to get them down but decided that would be too strenuous. I tried to ignore the cobwebs, but every time I went into the living room, my eyes would stray up to those disgusting offenders.

That afternoon, I also discovered that there was a halo of dust on the tops of all my curtains. Later that evening, my daughter called. She could tell from the tone of my voice that I was upset about something. I told her that I was frustrated because I needed to do some cleaning but thought that I should wait a day or two due to the surgery.

After I explained what I had discovered, she laughed. I was a little surprised and hurt, but she explained, "Mom, do you remember that I offered to get you a cleaning lady for your birthday?"

Of course, I remembered because I had told her in no uncertain terms "I am not that old, and I can certainly take care of my own house without help."

She said, "Well, now you know why I made you that offer."

I practically screamed into the phone, "You mean those cobwebs have been there that long?"

"Mom, I never noticed the cobwebs, but I had noticed the dust on the curtains and a few other things," she replied. "It's no big deal; you are just noticing because of your improved vision."

"It's a big deal to me. I've had friends over and now I'm embarrassed to have had a dirty home for them to see."

"They probably never even noticed, mom. Have any of them had cataract surgery yet?"

That made me laugh because my group of ladies had recently asked me all about just that subject when we were last together.

My daughter, bless her heart, came over a few days later and helped me take down the drapes. We almost choked on the dust, so I threw all my curtains away and went out to buy new ones. Earlier I had managed to pull down the cobwebs by myself.

A few months later, I had the cataract in the other eye removed too. Because I had one good eye, this time I drove myself to and from the surgery as it was only a few blocks away.

The change was not as dramatic as the first time, but I definitely noticed an improvement in my sight. Having two good eyes really made things clearer. The shock came the next day.

I had finished showering and was putting on makeup to go meet friends for lunch. Recently, I had started using one of those magnifying mirrors to make sure I get my makeup on right.

I was so shocked that I cried out. All I could see in that mirror were what seemed to be hundreds of wrinkles! Where had they come from?

Then I remembered that soon after my daughter's 40th birthday, she had asked me when I had noticed that I was getting wrinkles. She was worried about the changes usually connected to aging. But I had confidently told her that the women in our family were lucky as we didn't seem to age as much or as quickly as other women.

Now I know why she asked! I was fooling myself because I couldn't see clearly for years. Those wrinkles had been there all along.

I'm glad to have my vision back as I love to read and would feel really old if I couldn't drive myself around, but believe me, cataract surgery is a mixed blessing.

The Kilt

I have settled down as I got older, but sometimes my wilder side breaks though. It happened again a few years ago.

Some old friends had invited me out to Palm Springs as some of their friends from Japan had come for a visit. I spoke better Japanese than my friends, so they asked me to help bridge the language gap. It seemed that their Japanese visitors really wanted to go to the famous Gay Pride Parade and festival.

I usually avoid events where there are crowds of people, but since our visitors from Japan were set on this adventure, I said I'd join them. I didn't realize at the time how big an event this really is.

When I got there, I couldn't find a place to park anywhere near the parade route. I finally parked at a shopping center almost a half a mile from where I was to meet my friends.

As I walked towards the parade route, I could see a park across the street. As I got closer, I realized from the many signs that it was the site of the festival which opened after the parade. I looked at my watch and realized that I was probably too late to see most of the parade. My friends and their guests had planned on going to the festival when the parade ended.

I didn't have my cell phone with me. I trusted that they wouldn't change their plans and would show up at the festival after the parade. I was hot and tired, and so I went to the park entrance, found it open, paid the fee, and went in. I soon found a place to buy a cold bottle of water even though most concessions weren't open for business yet.

I wandered around looking at what the various stalls were offering. As I came around one corner, there was a booth selling kilts. Now these were American-made kilts, not the traditional kind from Scotland. They were not made of wool, but of denim and khaki and, of course, leather. I was curious, so I decided to look for a price tag on the rack nearest me.

Suddenly, there was a salesman by my side. Of course, he was wearing a kilt. He began his spiel about the quality and comfort of his company's kilts. Just to make conversation, I told him that I had recently read an article about how some blue-collar workers liked wearing kilts at work as they gave them freer movement than traditional work pants.

He whipped out a tape measure and had it around my waist before I could protest that I was only looking. He asked which material I liked best, but before I could say anything, he pulled out a tan khaki kilt and said, "Let's try this one on. It's definitely you."

The kilts snapped in the front, so he had that kilt around my waist before I could protest. I panicked and looked around for someone to help me get out of this predicament. Then I realized that there was absolutely no one anywhere near our area.

I chuckled when he said, "Well, this one is a little tight, and I don't know if I have this style in a bigger waist size." I thought that would put an end to it, but immediately he dropped to his knees in front of me and reached up under the kilt I had on.

If I had felt embarrassed before, now my face was beet red! He said, "Let's get your shorts off and see if it fits better." I was flabbergasted as he reached up, unsnapped, and unzipped my denim cutoff shorts and pulled them down. He stood up, adjusted the waistband again, and gave his approval of the fit. "That's better."

Then he led me to the back of the tent where there was a full-length mirror. I was shocked by what I saw. It actually looked good. I didn't look like I was wearing a 'girly' skirt. The kilt looked tailored, fitted, and professional, like a good pair of slacks.

He asked me if I would take that one or if I wanted to try on a different kilt. I stammered that it was probably more than I wanted to spend. I hadn't been able to find a price tag earlier. The price turned out to be about the same as a quality pair of slacks. As I looked in the mirror admiring my reflection, I couldn't believe that I was actually thinking about buying a kilt!

To buy some time, I asked him where I could change back into my regular shorts. He gave me a big smile and said that since I was his first customer, if I would agree to wear the kilt while I was at the festival, he would give me a 25% discount. I could never resist a bargain, so I bought a kilt!

I thought my friends would be surprised when they arrived at the festival and saw me in a kilt. Soon people began streaming into the festival as the parade ended. I walked around looking at all the other booths which were now open. After about an hour, I still hadn't seen my friends. Just as I was deciding to leave and was nearing the exit, I saw them coming in.

They had decided to go to lunch before coming to the festival. It took them about 10 minutes to notice that I was wearing a kilt (which made me feel better about buying it.) Then one of our Japanese guests wanted to buy one, so I led our group over to the booth.

The place was packed with people looking at kilts. As we waited to be served, we saw a number of people buying kilts. As they were fitted, they took off their shorts or jeans under the kilt as the salesman had done for me, but many also took off their underwear too!

I was struggling to explain to our Japanese friends in their language that traditionally in Scotland, no underwear was usually worn under a kilt. Immediately, one of our guests grabbed my kilt and lifted it up. I still had on my underwear, and everyone seemed disappointed–except me. I was just embarrassed.

I stayed for a while with our international guests, but since I had not eaten lunch, I was getting really hungry. Everything available at the festival was fast food and very expensive, so I said my goodbyes and left to find my car. I was so hungry that I pulled into the first restaurant I saw. I had forgotten I was still wearing the kilt. Surprisingly, no one seemed to notice my non-traditional outfit.

When I got home, I took the kilt off and laid it on the bed. I shook my head and wondered what I had been thinking. Now, every time I open the closet and see it in the back, I think, "Where would I ever wear that?"

Dealing With Grief

My German grandparents were married for over 50 years. They had retired from the farm and were living in a small town when my grandfather slipped on the ice on their front step, hit his head, and died. It was devastating to the whole extended family.

Grandma went into a depression. Since I lived nearby, I visited her almost every day to check up on her. She had a few lady friends from church also visiting her regularly.

One of them decided that Grandma should keep busy, so she taught her how to crochet. The first week or so after she learned the basics, she seemed to spend all her time unraveling what she had already done. She was always a perfectionist.

Once she mastered the technique, doilies, canister covers, table runners, etc. – anything she could find the pattern for in crochet magazines found its way into our homes. The whole family was overrun with crocheted gifts. Finally, one of my uncles told her to find some other activity.

So, she changed to knitting. Then we got mittens, blankets, and sweaters until we started running out of space to put them. One day, because she didn't drive, she asked me if I could drive her to the city to buy yarn. We came home with a carful of yarn! She was a regular cottage industry turning out products every day. Thank God she was also donating all kinds of things she made to the church's various charities.

Some months later, when I came into her house, I was swept away by the smell of something baking. She always was a good cook, and I suddenly realized that I hadn't smelled anything cooking in her house since Grandpa passed. I asked her what or who she was baking for, and she said she was going to enter some of her baking at the county fair.

I became her official taster for the next few weeks and probably gained 10 pounds. She went on to win first prize in all the categories that she entered, not only in baking, but also in crocheting and knitting. That was only the beginning. The next year she planted a garden and entered both her produce, and dishes made from what she grew, and of course, continued winning. She had a new outlook on life, and we stopped worrying about her being depressed.

The only time I saw her sad after that was when I took her to Christmas Eve services at her church. When the children came down the aisle holding candles in the darkened church, she sniffled a little, wiped her eyes, and told me that the children's procession was Grandpa's favorite part of the Christmas Eve service.

Family Frolics

Family means relatives, friends, comfort
food, fun events, or times when things
go sideways

The Birthday Surprise

As soon as I got out of the Marine Corps, I decided to stop shaving and getting my hair cut. I wanted to get as far away from that conservative world as possible. That didn't make my parents happy, to say the least, but at least I had a real job and had even bought my first home.

I was at the folks' house the weekend of my mother's birthday, and I decided to surprise her with a cake. Mom worked at the local dentist's office, so I could make a cake in her kitchen without interruption.

I had bought all the things I needed in the city before I went to my small hometown, so after I heard mom leave for work, I got up, ate a quick breakfast, and started making the cake.

As the box always tells us, the first thing to do is turn on the oven. I did that and then I went about mixing up the batter. My great aunt had run a bakery in a neighboring town, and I had picked up a few tricks from her, so this was going to be a special cake with fresh cherry pieces in it.

When I turned around to put the cake in the oven, I realized that the oven was cold. As I put the pans back on the counter, I wondered what was wrong. The oven at my house always lit immediately. Mom's house was on propane at that time, and I wondered if the tank was empty. I shrugged and looked around and found some matches.

I have to interject here that Mom's birthday is in February, and I had a cold and was all stuffed up and couldn't breathe through my nose. I turned the oven control off, and then I turned it back on and lit a match. What happened next was one of those amazing moments in life.

I swear that time slowed down. I saw a tiny spark jump from the end of the match and shoot straight into the oven. Then a huge wall of flame rolled back out at me.

I had just enough time to close my eyes. My natural instinct protected my eyes, but my eyelashes immediately melted together so I couldn't open my eyes.

There was the terrible smell of burned hair everywhere. I went into the bathroom, which was right off the kitchen, and splashed water on my face. I didn't feel burned, but I couldn't see. I realized I had no choice – I pulled out my eyelashes with a jerk.

That really hurt, but now I could see that my beard and hair had been singed all around my face. I also had no eyebrows. I looked surprised, which I certainly was.

Before I could think much about what had happened, I heard some noises coming from the kitchen. I went back into the kitchen. The curtains on the window beside the stove were on fire. I freaked out!

I jerked the curtains down along with the curtain rod and doused them in the sink. I then inspected the kitchen and could only see smoke damage; nothing else was on fire.

I went back into the bathroom and inspected myself. I wondered how I would be able to trim my mess of singed hair without cutting it all off.

Suddenly, I realized that most of my chest hair was gone too because I had not been wearing a shirt. I laughed and felt really grateful that I had put on pants before starting the cake!

I decided to call Mom and tell her not to come home for lunch, which she usually did. She asked why, of course, so I told her that I had made a big mess in the kitchen, and I wanted time to clean it up. I didn't give her any specifics.

I went back into the kitchen to start the cleanup and realized that the oven was indeed lit and warm. So, I put the cake in and finished baking it while I tried to clean up.

However, when I tried to wash the black soot off the walls, the old paint started to come off too. I realized then that I would have to come clean because the kitchen wouldn't!

With time on my hands, I finished Mom's special cake and it turned out great. In fact, I was just finishing the frosting when the door opened, and Mom came in.

I yelled from the kitchen to stay in the living room so I could bring the cake to her, but she smelled smoke and wanted to know just what was going on in her kitchen. She nearly fainted when she saw the state of the kitchen and my raggedy burned hair and beard.

I told her it wasn't as bad as it looked, and that I was going to repaint the whole kitchen for her. She had been trying to get Dad to let her remodel the kitchen for years, so she immediately started to see the possibilities with a new stove, new curtains, etc.

She called the insurance agent, and since his office was only a few minutes away, he came over immediately. He wrote up an estimate right there. Then we all sat down and had a piece of birthday cake. There was a lot of snickering whenever they looked up at my frizzled hair and beard.

Years later mom was telling the story to friends and said, "It turned out to be the best birthday present I ever had – I got a new stove and remodeled the kitchen – and he had to get his hair cut!"

A Seasonal Attitude Adjustment

My dad was the fourth of ten children born to Danish immigrant parents in Iowa at the beginning of the twentieth century. Unlike his three brothers, who became farmers, Dad went on to become a doctor.

After he graduated and settled down, he bought a house and built an office on one side of the house. When he was not in the office, he was at the hospital or driving around the county making house calls.

He maintained his farming roots, particularly when they had medical applications. "If you dig down beneath the snow, and come across little green shoots, then you know that that horseradish plant must have strong enzymes to survive the cold, so dig up some roots and use them as medicine when the flu season approaches." He also advised patients to start consuming local honey before the local hay fever season arrived.

Twenty years later, he built his dream house on top of one of the highest hills in town with a commanding view. He planted a large vegetable garden. After his three children grew up and moved away, he replaced the vegetable garden with his favorite Colorado blue spruce trees.

One snowy winter day, just a week or so before Christmas, as he was driving up the driveway, he saw that one of his beloved blue spruces had been cut down. He got out of the car and noticed fresh tracks in the snow. In a rage, he followed the tracks, trudging through the woods halfway around the hill, and then toward a poor neighborhood.

The tracks led him to a house, and presumably, to the culprit. He knocked on the door. A woman opened the door and asked,

"May I help you?" Behind her he caught a glimpse of children playing and laughing and decorating his blue spruce.

He paused, took a deep breath, and then turned to the woman and said, "I'm sorry. I must have the wrong address."

This story sums up how I remember my dad. I miss him and hope I have lived a life that would make him proud.

Bathroom Wars

When I was in college, some friends were sitting around one day talking about family, and when a friend learned that I had only one sister, she said, "Well, your house must have been pretty quiet." She had grown up with six siblings. I had to stop her right there and tell her about my daily fight for the bathroom.

My aunt worked at a sewing factory. She worked the early shift as she was up at the crack of dawn on the farm anyway to help with the chores and make breakfast for her husband and the kids. The early shift also let her get home soon enough to start dinner for the family.

From junior high school on, she dropped off my three female cousins at our house at about 5:30 a.m. They usually came in and sprawled on the furniture to get a little extra sleep until the rest of us got up about 6:30 a.m.

Then the house would come to life. There was breakfast to be had, clothes to be ironed, and for the girls, makeup to be put on and hair to be styled. All I wanted to do was eat my cereal, brush my teeth, comb my hair, and get out of the way, but it was never that easy.

I had to fight five women – my mother, my sister, and the three cousins – for the one bathroom in our house! Even Mom felt the pressure and had Dad put up a second mirror in the bathroom and another one on the enclosed back porch. That helped some, but when we were all in high school, the problem got really bad.

In the days of long straight hair, I could count on some time in the bathroom while the girls ironed each other's hair to make it perfectly straight. When big, back-combed, bouffant hairstyles came in, I hardly knew what the bathroom looked like; and if

I did get in there, I choked on the clouds of hairspray that lingered in there!

I started keeping my toothbrush and my own tube of toothpaste in my room so I could brush my teeth anywhere. I sometimes had to go outside to comb my hair in the side mirror of the car, and to be completely honest, sometimes I peed on the walnut tree in the back yard rather than try to get them out of the bathroom.

One day I needed to get into the bathroom for the usual reason – I actually had to go. The oldest of the cousins was hogging the mirror. She was by far the worst of the bunch as she spent lots more time on her makeup than the others.

Mom was already gone to work so there was no authority in the house. She wouldn't yield the bathroom. Since I knew that she was extremely ticklish, I decided that the only way to get her out of the bathroom was to tickle her.

The problem was that at that moment, she was curling her eyelashes. I didn't even know you could do that! She jumped, shrieked, and tore out most of her lashes on one eye. Instantly, she became hell's fury incarnate! She chased me around the house waving that eyelash curler like a lethal weapon.

Mom had already left for work and couldn't save me. I eventually escaped outside, but it was winter, and I didn't have my coat. I decided I'd wait in the garage until everyone left and then sneak back in to get my coat.

All the cousins and my sister had left to go to school – except the oldest! She wouldn't go to school with no eyelashes on one eye. Now what? I walked a couple of blocks to the convenience store to use their bathroom. A friend of my mom's worked there, and I told her the whole story.

She made a call and then sent me over to the beauty shop where I picked up a pair of glue-on lashes. I took them home as a peace offering, and while my cousin was trying to figure out how to use them, I grabbed my coat and ran to school, just in time for my first class.

We didn't see her at school until after lunch that day, and then everyone was complimenting her and saying that she looked really good. Years later, I found out that her first attempt to put on the fake lashes had glued one of her eyes completely shut, and it had taken most of the morning to get it unstuck.

She got the lashes on correctly on the second try. That first experience with those fake eye lashes must have really impressed her because to this day, she still wears fake eyelashes. I've never seen her without them.

Laughing in the Face o

There were three girls and one boy in our fai   ᵕ
a year or two apart in age, so we girls hung out to₂   ₁ ne boy
was the youngest and was spoiled by our parents. He was the
'wild child' of the family.

One year, our parents had family friends from another state
visit to celebrate the Day of the Dead with us. After a big dinner,
we kids were sent to the kitchen to do the dishes. The fact that
we had entertained company for dinner meant there was quite a
pile of dishes to get done.

We three girls organized the dishwashing. One would wash,
one would rinse, one would dry, and one would put things away.
Since our brother was younger and smaller, he couldn't put things
away in the cupboards, and we couldn't trust him to do a good
job washing or rinsing, so he got the job of drying.

We were just getting started with our little assembly line
when he started using the towel to snap us girls on the bottom.
We squealed and told him to stop, but he kept doing it. Before
we knew it, mom came in and told us to quiet down. We complained about our brother, and she told him to get serious about
the dishes.

As soon as she left, he started in again. The oldest sister
grabbed the towel and turned the tables on him. After she landed
a snap on his rear end, he started screaming and howling. The
door opened and this time, it was our father standing there with
a red face, threatening us with the 'belt.'

We knew that he was really mad, and that he was completely
serious. We tried to explain, but he said he didn't want to hear it
or any other sound from in here and stomped out.

˷ were quiet for a few minutes, but the 'wild child' never when to quit. He tried to get us with his towel a few more ˽nes. We glared at him and told him to stop. He just laughed and snapped the towel at us again. Finally, he landed a hit on my sister's behind, and she screamed in pain.

The door flew open, and there was dad. He said, "I warned you kids," and proceeded to unbuckle his belt and pull it out of the belt loops. We were scared that we were going to get a really bad whipping, but then his pants fell down around his ankles.

He was standing there in his old baggy underwear with a confused look on his face. We couldn't help it; we literally screamed with laughter. Dad looked more and more confused and embarrassed, and we kept rocking with laughter.

Mom appeared in the door and after taking in the situation, snorted, and tried to hold her own laughter in. She took ahold of Dad, pulled up his pants, and escorted him out of the kitchen.

She was back in a minute and told us to stop laughing because it made Dad feel bad and told us to finish the dishes. She turned to the 'wild child' and threatened him with being grounded permanently and with never being able to sit down again.

Smirking, we girls went back to our jobs, but occasionally, one of us would burst out laughing, remembering how our very real fear had turned into hysterical laughter. After that, any time Dad threatened to discipline us, we couldn't help but break out in laughter. Dad would swear and stomp off, shaking his head.

Pioneer Spirit

My aunt married a guy that the family didn't approve of because he didn't want to be a farmer and had other plans and ideas. They made a good life together, and after their kids were grown and gone, they retired and decided to prospect for gold in Alaska.

They moved up there and found jobs during the winter season. She worked part-time in a dentist's office, and he de-iced planes at the airport. In summer, they took leave from their jobs, got in their large, old camper van, and went out into the countryside.

He prospected for gold in the streams and rivers while she picked berries, wild herbs, and vegetables, and canned them. Of course, they also hunted and fished. My aunt even learned she could can salmon and moose, but her homemade wild blueberry jam was the best I ever tasted.

One summer they found a good place between the junction of two streams and set up their camp. They usually stayed in one place for at least a week or two to exhaust all the possibilities in that area.

My aunt was cooking down some blueberries for jam and doing the laundry. They had a small washer in a closet of the camper van. She had to carry the water from the stream for the washer, but she said it was better than beating the clothes on a rock. Of course, there was no dryer, so she just took the wet clothes out and spread them on the bushes to dry.

My aunt had just opened the closet door where the washer was and bent over to pull out a load of wet clothes when she heard a noise from the front of the van.

She yelled, "What are you doing back so early? Lunch isn't ready yet!" There was no answer, but she heard a strange scratching noise instead. She pulled her head out of the washer closet and looked around the door up the narrow hall.

There was a grizzly bear coming down the aisle. His nose was in the air sniffing, and when he got to the stove he stopped. My aunt slowly opened the closet door all the way to hide herself from the bear as much as possible.

She slowly backed towards the back door of the camper, and automatically reached for the rifle that hung in a rack alongside the door. She kept on backing up until she was outside.

She wanted to call out for my uncle but didn't know where he was. She listened but couldn't hear any sounds that might give her a clue as to where he might be.

As she was thinking about what to do, she heard the bear howl in pain. He had gotten into the hot blueberries and burned himself. Now the camper van started rocking and a horrible racket was coming from inside.

All my aunt could think was that the damn bear was tearing up her home, so she went back into the van through the back door yelling "You git!" and making all sorts of noise. She slammed the washer closet door violently, hoping to scare the bear.

Rather than running the other way, the bear turned and started shuffling right toward her. Instinctively, she lowered the rifle and shot. The bear took a few more steps, stopped, looked confused, and slumped to the floor. She had shot him exactly between the eyes at just the right angle. She had killed a grizzly with a .22 rifle!

About then, my uncle showed up. "What the hell is going on?" he yelled. As he came up into the front of the van and saw the bear, he said, "Why did you have to shoot it in here?"

My aunt glared at him and said, "I've got a couple more rounds in this rifle, so you'd better just shut up!" Then she burst into tears and slumped to the floor.

They drove the van to the nearest town 90 miles away and found some locals to help drag the bear out of the van. It took days to clean the camper up and try to find the parts to fix everything that the bear had torn up in just a few minutes.

That old van was never the same, and they never got the smell of bear completely out of it. But when my uncle said he was going to look for a replacement, my aunt blurted out that she wasn't sure that she want to get rid of it.

When he asked her why, she replied that the whole episode reminded her that she had the same spirit as her pioneer grandmothers, and it made her proud to know that she could face anything like they did.

Easter Shopping

In our church, Easter was a big holiday, and everyone bought new clothes for the celebration. The problem was that since Easter was a moveable date in the spring, and we lived in the Midwestern plains, we never knew if it would be warm and lovely, or freezing and blowing snow!

There weren't any clothing stores with much of a variety near our small town, so we would go to the bigger city nearby. It was Mom's big trip of the year. There were several large stores in the downtown area, and we would check them all out before deciding on our new spring outfits.

When my sister and I were in our early teens, we had an especially memorable shopping trip. We were in a more high-class store where we rarely bought anything unless it was marked down. That place had many floors and an escalator in the center going up and down.

We took the escalator up one floor, and there was a group of mannequins right as we got off the escalator. I felt that it was just natural to reach out and shake the hand of the nearest one, who seemed to be welcoming us to the floor. Unfortunately, the mannequin's hand came off in my hand. Mom was not amused.

"Quick, put it back on!" she said. I tried but it just wouldn't go back on, so I tucked it in the only place to hide it, her boat-necked blouse. Unfortunately, one finger caught on the edge of the neckline, so there were a few fingertips peeking out of her blouse. My sister cackled and mom cracked up but pulled us away from there before someone came along to see what was wrong.

She was shaking her head and muttering to herself as we headed around to take the escalator up to the next floor. As we were going up, I was sort of hanging over the edge of the escalator and my elbow accidentally caught the wig of a mannequin on that side. The wig flipped onto the floor. Mom quickly looked to see if anyone had seen it. No one had, so we put on serious faces and went on up.

Later, coming back down the escalator, mom saw some item that she wanted to look at. Coming down an escalator always has you facing in the opposite direction than going up, so we didn't realize that we were the floor where I had wreaked havoc on the mannequins.

On our way to the escalator down to the next floor, we passed the bald mannequin. I saw that the wig was still on the floor where it had landed, so I picked it up and tried to put it back on. I was much shorter than the mannequin, and I did my best, but the wig somehow slipped up and over the bald head and disappeared down the escalator shaft.

Mom was furious and was cursing about not being able to take me anywhere. When she rounded the corner to go down the escalator, there was the mannequin with the hand crawling out of the top of her blouse. It was too much–we all exploded with laughter.

Mom dragged us over to the elevator (which she never liked to use) and luckily an empty one arrived immediately. She ordered us to straighten up and not embarrass her as we made it to the ground floor.

We had almost made it to the door nearest the escalators when just as we were about to escape, we saw a confused floor clerk with a wig in his hands. He was walking around looking at all the mannequins to see which one had lost its hair.

We erupted in laughter once again. We made it out the door to the street and finally escaped.

How I Found Another Family

I was new to Honolulu, just starting graduate school, and I didn't know many people. I only knew one other meditation teacher that I had met at a retreat. I went with him to my first teachers' meeting at the meditation center in downtown Honolulu.

When we came up the stairs, there were quite a few people standing around talking. My friend immediately went off to speak to some friends.

A lady came up and asked if she could help me. After I explained to her that I was new in town, and that my friend had told me about the meeting, she, and everyone else were quite welcoming.

I told them I was a grad student at UH Manoa, and a guy guided me across the room to meet another person from the college. It turned out to be one of the professors I had just met that week!

He was surprised and glad to see me, and when someone called "Let's get started," he led me into the meeting hall. We sat near the back of the hall, and I occasionally asked him a question about who was speaking and their position in the meditation center.

Suddenly, a red-headed girl who was sitting directly in front of us turned around and said, "Would you be quiet, please? We're trying to hear what they're saying." I thought she was a little rude, but we stopped talking.

Then during most of the meeting, she talked incessantly to the woman sitting next to her rather than listening! I looked at the professor, but he just shook his head, so I didn't say anything about the woman's hypocritical behavior.

That was my first introduction to Laura who, many years later, is like a sister to me. We still don't see eye-to-eye on many subjects, but we have a deep and lasting connection.

Laura had a younger sister, Sherry, who had been married but was leaving her husband and moving in with their parents. A little later, I found out that Laura was moving to New Zealand to live with her new boyfriend. So, after I had worked a few weeks at the meditation center, Laura decided that Sherry should take the advanced course that I had been assigned to teach at the center.

Sherry was shy and a little depressed when I first met her, but she was a kind and gentle soul. We both enjoyed the experience of interacting with the 20 other people who were enrolled in the course.

When Thanksgiving came around, Sherry realized that I knew almost no one else in Hawaii, so she invited me to come to her parents' home for dinner. Of course, I went, as the idea of spending the holiday alone was depressing.

I was met at the screen door on the porch by a large Dalmatian dog who was growling something fierce, though his tail was wagging. Since I have always had a good relationship with dogs, I opened the screen door and patted him on the head.

He responded by jumping up on me with his paws on my shoulders, drowning me with dog slobber! Just then, Sherry's folks came out of the kitchen, laughed, and helped me wipe off my face.

The fact that the dog liked me, and that I had correctly interpreted his growling as a welcome, made me an instant member of the family. In Hawaii, there is a custom of adopting people into families, so over the next 10 years, we became a close family. I was the son that they had never had, and they were the warm, loving, encouraging parents that my own family had never been. Having a family like them made my time in Hawaii a true adventure in paradise.

We all lived happily together for a number of years before everyone left Hawaii for different reasons. Even though we lived in different parts of the U.S., we kept in touch and visited as often as we could. Our love for each other only deepened over the years, and I still remember some of those times as the most important experiences in my life.

They are all gone now, except for Laura, who started it all with a snippy comment and rude chatter all those years ago. How different my life would have been if she hadn't come into my life, bringing with her a wonderful loving family who changed my life for the better.

Just Being Practical

The phone rang. It was my mother. I didn't feel up to chatting with her after work, so I let it go to the answer machine.

"Come to brunch on Sunday. We have to have a family conference. Your sister's coming too. I'm making fried chicken with all your favorites, so don't tell me you're not coming," was the message she left.

I wondered what this was all about. On the other hand, I really loved my mom's cooking. I was on a diet, but we did have one 'free' day a week. Of course, I went and as usual, I took some mending as I never could sew very well, and it made mom feel more useful to still take care of us girls.

The brunch went as usual with my sister and I catching the folks up on our lives and enjoying the home-cooked meal.

When the chatter came to a natural break, my mother said, in a normal conversational tone, "Just so you know, I've got breast cancer–stage two. I'm scheduled for surgery next week."

It hit my sister and I like a punch in the gut. Suddenly we were talking over each other trying to get more information. At first, Mom tried to put us off by saying that she had really good doctors, and that they had caught it fairly early.

My sister told her that we needed more specific information as her cancer would now be hanging over our heads as sometimes it is a genetic condition that can be passed on.

Mom sat there for a moment, and it was obvious that she had not even thought of that before. Finally, she shook her head and said, "OK, what do you want to know?"

The first thing my sister said was "How did you find out?"

Mom looked up quickly at Dad and blushed. "Well, your father found the lump first." Then Dad blushed, and we all burst out laughing.

That broke the ice and eventually, we got all the answers to all the questions we could think of, but Dad wouldn't make eye contact with either of us all afternoon.

The mastectomy surgery went well and after some time, Mom was declared cancer free.

Mom was just in her sixties, but she didn't opt for the usual reconstructive implants. She thought having something foreign put permanently into your body was gross.

My sister and I went with her to explore options for bra fillers. We looked at two types: one was a sort of pillow made of natural materials and the other was a molded gel-filled silicone model. Since she couldn't make up her mind, she ended up buying one of each.

Mom had always thought that it was important to be well-dressed. She soon decided that the silicone boob was for going out in public, and the more comfortable pillow boob was for everyday use around the house.

A couple of years later, I went to Mom's to pick up some new clothes that she was hemming for me. She was upstairs sitting at the sewing machine just finishing when I came in the room.

As she moved, I saw something glint on her chest. When I looked closely, I saw that she had several straight pins sticking out of her chest!

"Mom! What the hell?"

She looked down and then said with a gleam in her eye, "You see? I found a good, practical use for that pillow boob."

Holiday Food Rituals

Some of the most important family rituals in our lives revolve around the food served at certain holidays. When I lived in Hawaii, I met a wonderful family who took me in and called me their adopted son. Being a part of their family made my life in a strange place much nicer, but it also meant learning a lot of new family traditions.

I was surprised at Thanksgiving by some of the dishes which they thought were absolutely necessary to properly celebrate the holiday. All my life, I had heard about succotash, but I had never seen it or tasted it. It didn't taste bad, but it was not what I was used to. That ritual came from the parents' childhood in Florida and Louisiana. That season also introduced me to okra cooked in several different ways–fried in bacon grease with freshly chopped tomatoes was my favorite.

We also had to have baked spaghetti! I had never heard of such a thing. It had no tomato sauce, only melted cheese and spaghetti. It was a lot like macaroni and cheese only messier.

This dish seemed completely removed from everything I knew about Thanksgiving. It turned out that the father's parents had been missionaries in South America and had picked up a taste for this dish, (called *fideos hornos* in Spanish) and they had added it to their annual ritual meal.

We all helped cook for these giant feasts, so my contribution came from an aunt who had lived in Southern California for many years. At her Thanksgiving table, the sweet potatoes were cooked, mashed, blended with a little orange juice, put back into orange peel halves and popped in a hot oven to melt a marshmallow on the top of each one. They loved it.

When Christmas came around, we sang every carol we could think of. Of course, we had been drinking some strong eggnog and eating chocolate bourbon balls (another southern family tradition).

In my own family, the ritual I liked best was celebrating birthdays. For our birthday, my grandmother would make us any kind of cake we wanted. She was a famous baker in those parts, and her sister was a well-known cake decorator at the local bakery. Grandma had recipes for all kinds of cakes. She would spread them all out on the big kitchen table and let us decide which we wanted. They were all good, so it was always a win/win situation.

Instead of asking for a particular kind of cake, you could also ask for a theme cake. My older cousin asked for a baseball cake. Grandma and Aunt Lulu created an amazing cake with a baseball diamond and bleachers and all the players. My cousin didn't want them to cut it up, but what good is a cake if you don't eat it!

As we gained more and more cousins over the years, she would make two or three cakes so that we could all have a piece to help the cousins celebrating a birthday.

When I was living in Japan, I discovered some new food rituals. For instance, everyone is supposed to have noodles on New Year's Eve to signify the wish for long life (like the long noodles.)

Whatever food ritual you and your community have adopted, they are important for the continuity of the group and often serve to teach important lessons – like the seder dinner in Jewish tradition. They are also a great way to make new friends and discover new tastes.

Driving with Mom

My Mother was the designated driver long before the term existed. She started driving to help out on the farm during harvest season. Even though she was the second child, Mom drove herself and her older and younger sisters six miles to the high school nearest the farm. Most of the way the roads were dirt or, more specifically, mud. Grandpa ended up keeping three Model T Fords during those years – one for them to drive, one for parts, and one in the shop being rebuilt for use the next year!

During the bad parts of the year, the dirt roads would get deep ruts in them. Sometimes the ruts were so deep that the car would drag, and the girls would have to get out and push. Once in a while, the car would take off without them, but they knew it would slow down and stop going up the next hill, and it couldn't get out of the ruts anyway!

They always had two sets of clothes with them in case they got dirty getting to school in situations like this. They also carried a ten-gallon milk can full of water to soften the mud that collected on the fenders. So much mud would build up that they would have to stop and remove it so that they could go on.

When the oldest sister had graduated, Mom drove to school with her younger sister. By that time, part of the road to town had been paved. That meant that they could drive faster on that part of the road.

One day, just as they were coming around the curve into town, a back wheel came off and passed them. It went off into the brush along the road and into the creek! That was a little hard to explain.

Since Mom was one of the cheerleaders and the games were often at night, she and her sister took a room in town for part of the year when the weather was bad. They were not supposed to use the car to go anywhere but school, but of course they went to dances, parties, and out of town games.

In order for Grandma and Grandpa not to find out that they had been using the car more than they were supposed to, they spent hours driving the Model T around town backwards to take the miles off the speedometer. Later their younger brother showed them how to disconnect the speedometer.

When Mom graduated and married, she still drove a lot still helping out on the farm even after she had kids. When I was just a little kid, probably three or four years old, we lived in the country on a gravel road. The only problem with gravel was that over the year the gravel all moved off to the side of the road, so every spring the road grader would come around and push all the gravel back into the center of the road, then spread it out on the main surface again.

One day my mom needed to go to town to get something, so she packed up my sister, who was still a baby, and me. We headed for the nearest town. We had only gone a short way when she saw that the gravel on the road ahead was piled up in the middle. The road grader wasn't anywhere to be seen. Mom was in a hurry, so she tried to go around the gravel by moving over to the shoulder.

Now this part of the road had fairly deep ditches on each side. The car tilted dangerously, but she kept on going. The car started sliding into the ditch, so she gunned the motor, hoping to creep up the slope a little. However, the tires lost traction and we slipped all the way down the slope into the deep ditch.

The car was at such an angle that the driver's side door was too heavy for my mom to push open and the passenger's side door was up against the ditch. So, we waited.

Finally, the road grader came along and stopped. He didn't have any chains to pull us out with, so he went to the nearest house and called into town. Pretty soon, a guy came out with a truck, but he had to wait until the grader had flattened down the gravel before he could pull us out.

When my dad got home that day, he asked my mom if she had had a good day. She didn't want to tell him what had happened, but he already knew because it was the talk of our small town. He definitely wasn't happy when he got a bill for the towing.

The Hurricane Turkey

Growing up in the Midwest, I was used to fifteen-minute weather segments on the evening news. You can imagine my surprise when I found out that in Hawaii, they didn't even have a weather segment. They just said – "Tomorrow will be another beautiful day in Paradise!" The weather was not news – usually.

It was November and I was in graduate school at the University of Hawaii. We were going into the short Thanksgiving week, which was the sign that the semester would soon be over.

Monday was an unusual day. There were very high clouds making the day a little cooler than usual, and the trade winds were a little stronger than usual. That night on the news, they finally did talk about the weather.

It seemed a hurricane was moving towards the islands. This only happens about once every fifteen years or so. Hawaii is in a charmed location – all the storms either pass to the north or the south of the islands.

On Tuesday, the sky was a little cloudier and the winds a little stronger, nothing too bad, but by noon the word had come down that school was closing for the rest of the week. I thought that this was a little reactionary as it didn't seem that bad to me, but then people there didn't get many big storms, so they were a little panicky.

I called my adopted folks and told them that my friend Mary and I would be out on Wednesday – a day early for Thanksgiving. They asked me to pick up some charcoal, bottled water, and flashlight batteries on the way, just in case.

The storm picked up strength all day on Wednesday. I had never seen the wind blow so hard or the surf be so big on the west shore of O'ahu.

There were long lines at the stores, so it took me more than an hour just to get a few items. As we drove around the island to get to the folks, I could feel the wind pushing against my small Toyota, and the wind was full of sand.

Mary asked if we were on a different road. When I asked why, she said that she had never noticed a beach on her side of the car – that's how much sand was blowing across the road!

That night we could hear the wind howling outside and occasionally hear palm fronds crash to the ground. At about ten, Mary and I went to take the dog out for a short walk. The wind was so strong and full of sand that we didn't get far before deciding to go back, and the dog didn't object either.

The sound of the surf was deafening. I went back in and told everybody to come out and listen. The surf was crashing on the highway and sloshing up the street! We were scared! The beach was only a few short blocks from the house.

We looked around to make sure things that could be damaged by water were up and out of the way. We had already tied things down that could have been caught in the wind. The water never made it into the yard, but the wind carried tons of sand through the streets that night.

Just as we got back inside, the electricity went out. We sat around with candles and talked for a while, and then went to bed. We didn't sleep very well that night.

The wind was wild and since most windows in Hawaiian homes are slatted louvers, there was a strong breeze inside the house. There was also a lot of noise from things blowing and banging around.

On Thanksgiving morning, all was still. We found out from the transistor radio that the storm had moved swiftly away but the island was paralyzed. Since the folks lived in an out-of-the-way place, we realized that the electricity would most likely be out for several days.

Mom had been up early making all the fixings for the turkey dinner on the gas stove that ran off a propane tank. She had prepared all the other traditional holiday food first and was at last ready to stick the turkey in the oven about 9:00 a.m. We expected to eat around 2:00 that afternoon.

About 11:00, she went to check the turkey and found it cold. Their propane tank was empty! We decided that only thing we could do was cook the turkey on the barbecue grill.

We started up the fire, wrapped the turkey in foil, and sat back and waited for it to cook. In an hour, we needed to relight the fire as it had all burned down. We kept testing the turkey, but it never seemed to be cooking very well.

Eventually, we ate all the side dishes one by one because we were hungry: the stuffed celery, the sweet potatoes, the succotash, the giblet stuffing, even the pumpkin pies – all cold, of course.

To keep our spirits up, we played board games and invented some new Thanksgiving cocktails. Later, I had to walk down to the local store to buy more charcoal.

The store was open, but they couldn't open the cash register, so people just gave them cash. They were good people and weren't charging more than the marked price rounded up to the nearest dollar.

There was a line when I got there, and I'm sure they sold out of almost everything. I only had $20 bills from the ATM, so I ended up buying chips and dip and cookies, as well as several big bags of charcoal just to bring the total up. Nobody complained when I got back to the house as we were all still a little hungry. By then we had eaten anything left in the refrigerator that didn't need cooking.

That turkey used up five big bags of charcoal and it wasn't ready until almost 7:00 that night, but when it was done, it was fantastic! It was one of the best turkeys I've ever eaten. It was fall off the bone tender and very juicy, but I never want to wait that long for any meal again!

Christmas Dinner at Grandma's

I am so glad to be at Grandma's for Christmas dinner. The house smells so good! I can smell that the turkey is already out of the oven and cooling. I cruise the kitchen and sneak a taste of the rich giblet dressing.

I can also smell the pumpkin pies baking. Grandma is making a terrific noise mashing the potatoes. I catch a glimpse of my aunt's pineapple fluff dessert, which is my favorite, before the kids are shooed out of the kitchen.

More cousins pour in from the cold outside. It's snowing lightly, so we are told we need to stay inside and play in the parlor. The giant wood stove crackles and pops. The room is hot near the stove and cooler near the windows and doors.

We kids play Alligator, running and jumping from chair to chair to sofa while the oldest cousin is on the floor on his knees trying to catch us.

Shouts and screams of joy echo through the house, and one of the aunts comes in to tell us to stop and help set up the folding tables. It's chaos as we all try to help setting the table. Everyone is in everyone's way as there are fifteen of us cousins now.

The grownups' table is beautifully set with the cloth that came from Germany long ago with our great great grandma. We all have to wait for Grandma, who has gone upstairs to change into her best dress. We kids crowd together behind the adults for grace.

Grandpa delivers the prayer, and some others give additions, and then it is time to eat! We are holding our plates during grace so that we can fill them up before we go back to the parlor. The little kids give their plates to their parents, but us bigger kids get to serve ourselves. We get apple cider as a special treat.

We stuff ourselves. Everything tastes great, but I always love Grandma's fragrant, homemade rolls. I eat them first while they are still warm, dripping with butter and Grandpa's clover honey.

Later, after lots of stories and laughter, we have dessert. Great grandma then comes around the table with a big bowl full of whipped cream. She always asks, "Mit Schlag?" but it doesn't matter whether you say 'yes' or 'no'; she covers whatever you have chosen from the enormous spread of desserts under a white cloud of whipped cream.

Later we get our Christmas presents. Grandpa gives each of us kids a silver dollar, and grandma hands out an orange from California to all of us kids.

Now the snow is coming faster, and the wind is picking up. Those who live the farthest away leave first. The fathers go out and warm up the cars, while the mothers pack up baskets of leftovers and sort out the bowls and silverware that they brought.

We kids struggle into our coats, hats, and boots. The older ones help the little ones get dressed for the cold outside. I don't want to leave, but I know that there are more presents for me at home under our tree.

School Daze

We all lived through (and mostly enjoyed) the craziness of our classes, teachers, and classmates.

Speech Class Uproar

Speech was my favorite subject in high school. I have never had stage fright. I didn't understand what happened to friends who got all weird when it came time to perform in front of people.

When Danny joined our speech class a week late, it was a little surprising. Also, he was one year older than the rest of the class. The teacher told us that he hadn't graduated with the rest of his class because he lacked a few units, but if he passed this class, he would get his diploma.

Most of us hardly knew him because he was one of the quietest guys in school. The teacher was obviously trying to make it easy for him because she told us not to laugh or make him feel embarrassed since he was very shy.

Our first assignment was a simple report. We were to take an article out of a newspaper or magazine and pretend that we were TV reporters and give the information like on the evening news. All was going well until Danny's turn came. He was reporting on a fire in a neighboring town. The problem was his pronunciation.

Apparently, he was not familiar with one word in his report. He kept mispronouncing the word 'warehouse.' Instead of pronouncing the first syllable with the 'where' sound, he kept saying it like 'war.' Because he kept looking down at his paper and his voice was rather soft, we all thought he said "whore house!" In his report, he had to repeat that word a number of times.

Of course, we all wanted to laugh, but tried valiantly not to. We were all about to explode from choking back our laughter when we noticed that the teacher had her head down on the desk. The back of her neck was bright red, and she was shaking slightly. We were afraid that she was angry as she was a very religious woman. She never wore makeup, and her dresses were ultraconservative–sleeves to her wrists and hems to her ankles.

When Danny finally finished (it felt like fifteen minutes but was only a few minutes), there was a very pregnant silence for a moment, and then the teacher raised her head and laughed like a mad woman. That set the rest of us off. It was deafening in that room for about 5 minutes while Danny's face got redder and redder.

Finally, she raised her hand and we settled down. Then she said that she would have to give Danny an 'A' for the funniest report of all, and she thanked him for giving us all a good laugh.

After class, he asked me what had started the whole thing, and when I told him about his pronunciation mistake, he was so embarrassed that he didn't want to go back to class. The teacher finally convinced him that it was all right, and that no one would ever mention it again.

One of the other assignments for that class was to tell a joke. I worked with Danny on that assignment. He seemed to understand that pacing and timing were really important for a joke to work, but when he got in front of the class, his stage fright kicked in again.

He recited the joke as fast as he could in a monotone, and of course, no one laughed. He stood there for a few seconds, and then said, "I guess I'm only funny when I screw up." The class exploded in laughter, and although Danny got red, he also smiled back at us.

It worked out well. Danny opened up; we all became good friends. He passed the class and graduated.

My Cleverness Unmasked

What is embarrassing to some may not be embarrassing to others. This is not just true for the bigger cultural gaps between countries, but also for family cultures that might be quite different. My own farming family is rarely embarrassed about anything.

When I was teaching, I had a habit of sitting on the edge of my desk while I talked to the class. It gave me a better view of all the students. My desk was near the front of the room and fairly close to the blackboard.

One day during a discussion of some sort, I was asking a student on one side of the room a question. He was having some trouble coming up with an answer, but from the other side of the room, a student answered my question correctly.

I spun around and jumped off the desk to write the answer on the board, but as I did, I let a small fart. It was what my grandfather would have called a 'squeaker'. Fearing some students might be offended by farting, I concocted a clever cover up story.

I made a comment about the desk getting old and squeaky, and joked about the desk complaining because I was too heavy for its old legs to hold. I then wrote the answer on the board, and we went on with the lesson as if nothing unusual had happened.

I really thought that I had gotten away with it – until years later when I was in Japan and met up with one of the students who had been in that class. We went to a restaurant in Tokyo and reminisced about his experiences in the USA.

At one point he said that one of the funniest things that he remembered was the day I farted in class. I played dumb and said that he must have me confused with one of the other teachers.

However, he related the story exactly as it had happened – even remembering my excuse!

He said that the students had gotten together in the cafeteria after class to laugh about it. He told me that they thought it was very funny not because I farted, but because I blamed it on the desk!

I guess I wasn't as clever as I thought!

Suddenly Aging

I have been an educator all my professional life. I feel blessed to have had a job that I enjoyed and looked forward to every day. I have always taught young adults from many countries just entering college.

Being a bachelor without a family of my own, I came to think of my students as my kids. I was often a parental substitute for them, giving advice, encouragement, and sometimes an appropriate scolding.

Through the years, I met some very special students, and we felt a deeper connection. At some point, our roles changed, and these former students became friends. We kept in contact, and they often invited me to visit them in their home countries. Since I had the time and money, I sometimes took them up on their kind offers.

As they married and started their own families, I became the "crazy American" uncle to kids in many countries. I have seen my former students' kids grow up as I visited over the years, and I have even taught the son of one of my former students in the same English as a Second Language school that he went to 20 years before.

Now that I'm retired, I have more time to go on international adventures. A few years ago, I visited one of the more recent students who had become a friend and met his wife and four-year old son. The boy immediately attached himself to me, and I was deeply moved by his affection for me. When his bedtime came and his mother tried to take him upstairs for his bath and bed, he cried and clung to me.

Since I was staying overnight with them, his mother explained that he would see me in the morning. He was still not completely convinced, and turned and asked his mother in German if "grandfather" could come upstairs and help tuck him in.

Since I speak some German, I understood what he had said but was confused. Why was he talking about his grandfather who lived in another city? Then it dawned on me that he was talking about me! Suddenly, I was no longer the "uncle;" now I was the "grandfather!"

It only took me a moment to make that change of roles in my mind, and I gratefully accepted my new status. Later I learned that I was actually older than his real grandfather.

Each year in my classes, the kids never got older, and I never felt older either. Now that I'm retired, I wonder, when did I get so old?

Many Schools—Many Lessons

The other day I heard a song called "Home," in which the singer longs to go back to his home. It reminded me that my family moved often, so I went to many schools. In each place, I learned a lesson not taught in the classroom.

The first place I remember was a farm. I started kindergarten there. There were 8 students counting myself. I had to walk three-quarters of a mile to a one-room country schoolhouse. There was one tree out in the schoolyard which the boys often climbed in during recess.

During recess, one of the older boys 'helped' me up the tree. I was afraid, but he said he'd get me down. However, he left me up there when it was time to go back in. When class was supposed to begin, the teacher noticed I was not there. When she came out to look for me, I said "Hi, teacher!" from my perch in the tree. She helped me down and scolded the boys for leaving me there. I learned not to trust those who seemed friendly but were hiding their true intentions.

From that farm, we moved to a small village. The school was just up the hill from our house, and my first-grade class had their own room and teacher. We had a nice big playground for recess. I fell in love with a red-haired girl in the third grade. I yelled "You're pretty," at her, and was devastated when she turned to look and fell out of the swings and broke her arm. I learned to be careful to not hurt the ones you love.

My family then moved to a farm in Missouri. I had to ride a bus to school in the village which was about twelve miles away. It was another one-room, one-teacher school although much bigger than the first one I went to.

I went to second and third grade there. Our class, which had only 4 people in it, got to go up to the table in the front once in the morning and once in the afternoon for our lessons. I was a talkative, bothersome student. I was bored with our own lessons, and I often interrupted the lessons of other classes with questions. The teacher ignored me most of the time to keep order and to get through the lessons for all the other classes.

One day I suddenly had to go to the bathroom really bad. The rule in that school was to hold up your hand and get permission. The teacher either didn't see me or ignored my hand in the air. It was an attack of diarrhea, and I soon couldn't hold it any longer, and I pooped my pants right there in my seat.

I was so embarrassed that I put my head down on my desk and cried. Soon the smell caused one of the other students near me to raise her hand and complain to the teacher.

The teacher said that I should have just gone to the bathroom since it was an emergency. I stayed in the boy's bathroom most of that day as the diarrhea didn't let up, and I was too embarrassed to face the other students. I learned that the rules sometimes have to be broken.

A few years later, we moved back to the town where I was born when I was halfway through the fourth grade. The other students were ahead of me in learning the multiplication tables and it was hard to catch up. I was also sick a lot and missed classes. That teacher did not help me catch up. I had always been the star student, so I was crushed by her treatment of me. I realized later that by ignoring me, she had taught me that I could learn independently without a teacher. Learning was up to me not the teacher. That lesson helped me a lot in later life.

We moved into a much bigger house on the other end of town the next year. I remember that my room had a window that you could crawl out of and be right on the roof. One time we had a party with some other neighbor kids. We were eating watermelon on the roof and spitting the seeds as far as we could from the roof.

The neighbor lady saw us and yelled at us to get down. My friend Billy was so scared that he tried to hurry down. He stepped on some watermelon seeds and was gone over the side of the roof in a split second. He landed in my mother's flower bed, so he only got the wind knocked out of him. He got up and ran home, leaving a big hole in mom's prize garden. I learned that somebody is always watching you and to be careful.

In that same house, I poured Cheerios down the furnace vent because I wanted the toy in the bottom of the box. Since it was summer when I did it, no one found out. Of course, when cold weather came and the furnace came on for the first time, it blew Cheerios all over the kitchen, and I was in deep trouble. I didn't know the term at the time, but this was my first lesson about karma–all actions have inevitable reactions.

My family bought a different house when I was in Junior High. My dad built me a bedroom in the basement. I had all the privacy that I needed as I went through puberty. In high school, I really liked getting to choose the classes that I wanted.

As most people know, education doesn't only take place in school. I got drunk for the first time when I was a senior in high school. I passed out at a party, and my friends were worried about taking me home because it was after midnight, and they didn't want to face my dad. My friends used lots of mom's clothes pins to attach my big, baggy jacket (with me in it) to the clothesline behind our house. That is where my folks found me sound asleep the next morning. Dad just laughed. I learned that you can't always predict how people will act–even those you think you know well.

So where is this home that guy is singing about? Several of the houses we lived in are now completely torn down. I think the home he is singing about is more of a feeling than an actual place.

I have lived and gone to schools in many places, all of which have taught me valuable lessons.

Every place changes over time. Maybe we can never go back home physically, just in our memories. Each place and experience is a piece of the puzzle which makes up who we are.

Open Mouth, Insert Foot

When I went to my first college English class, I sat next to a cute girl who was very friendly. She told me her name was Cindy. It turned out that we lived in the same very large dorm complex that had a men's building and a women's building.

There were 800 students in the two buildings, and we shared some facilities like the cafeteria. I worked in the kitchen on a scholarship, and occasionally saw Cindy pass through the line out front.

We often talked just before class, mostly about the assignments or the weather, because our classroom was in an old campus building that was either too hot or too cold.

Just before the winter holiday break, the dorm administrators threw a party for all the students in the cafeteria. I went and was happy to see Cindy across the room. I started over to greet her as she was one of the few people I knew in the vast crowd.

She was happy to see me, and we were chatting about our holiday plans when a guy came by and asked her where her other half was. I figured she had a boyfriend when she said, "Oh, around here somewhere."

A girlfriend of hers came by, and they got to talking about some other class she was taking. I was just sitting there thinking that maybe I should leave before her boyfriend showed up.

Then I looked toward the door, and I had a 'Twilight Zone' moment. There was Cindy coming toward me with a big smile on her face. I was freaked because I knew that she was still sitting right beside me. I turned to look at her and she must have seen the look on my face because she asked, "What's wrong?"

I was so flustered that I couldn't even answer. I just turned to look at the other Cindy who was still bearing down on me. Cindy followed my look and then said, "Oh, gosh. I never told you I had a twin."

Her sister was an identical twin, and they were dressed in the same outfit! As the other sister came up to us, she introduced herself, "Hello, I'm Sandy Klaus."

I thought it was some sort of holiday joke that she was trying to pull on me, so I stood and said, "Nice to meet you. I'm Mary Christmas!"

She stared at me like I had lost my mind. Then Cindy said, "Oh my God, I never even told you my last name. It's Klaus with a K. We're Cindy and Sandy Klaus."

I wanted the floor to open up and swallow me at that moment, but with one girl hanging on each arm, they sat me down, and we all had a real good laugh about it.

Breakfast Epiphany

I went to college on scholarships because my folks didn't have the money to pay for my schooling. One of my work/study scholarships was working in the dorm cafeteria. Since I have always been an early riser, I chose the breakfast shift. That meant that I was getting up at 5 a.m. in order to be at work at 5:30 a.m.

For most of the first year, my work partner was a guy named Don. He was African American, or as we said in those days – Black. He was a great guy and we worked well together. I often stopped by his room on the way to the kitchen early in the morning to make sure he was up.

We were never very awake or talkative over our cereal, which we ate before going back into the kitchen to get things ready for the 200 students that regularly showed up for breakfast. One morning, the bowl that contained the sugar packets was not on the table. Since I ate one of the presweetened cereals, I hadn't noticed the sugar was missing from the table. Don always ate Grape Nuts and needed the sugar.

He sort of grunted at me to get him the sugar from the table behind me. Without looking up or thinking, I said what I had heard my father say many times in our house, "Who was your nigger waiter last year?"

As soon as I realized what I had said, I panicked. I thought that I would never use the N-word, but there it was, in the middle of a stock phrase that I had heard members of my family use for years to mean "I'm not your slave."

I'm sure that my family had never even thought about what they were saying. I was so embarrassed that I wanted to drop off

107

the face of the Earth. This was a guy that I really thought of as a friend! How could I have insulted him like that?

I started to stammer out an apology when he burst out laughing. He laughed so hard that he almost choked, while I was feeling so low that I could have crawled under the table.

I apologized to Don every time that I saw him for weeks until he told me to stop as it was embarrassing him. He realized that I didn't mean it the way it sounded, and, in fact, he said that he had never heard that saying before. It really meant nothing to him as an upper middle-class kid.

Well, it meant something to me! I became much more vigilant of the words and phrases I used, and even found a few other expressions that I purposely removed from my vocabulary.

I came to realize how insidious racism and other prejudices can be – we might not even know that they are there if we don't look carefully.

Months later, Don told me that he had told the story to his whole family over a holiday dinner. He said that his grandmother, whom he respected greatly, listened carefully, thought a moment, and then said, "He must be a good friend if he doesn't even remember that you're black!"

She somehow knew that I would never have said anything to hurt my friend Don, and that it was a slip of the tongue. In the end, it made our friendship even closer, and the next year, we became the first students of different races to share a dorm room breaking an old taboo at our university.

Finding Myself

I was sort of shy as a kid – at least around people that I didn't know, or those who didn't like me for some reason. My shyness was a kind of protective bubble. That bubble allowed me to feel that I didn't have to interact with others.

Occasionally, that bubble would burst. I remember one day in junior high school. We had to line up for lunch on the school stairs that wound up three floors. I was waiting to get into the lunch hall, talking to one of my friends, when *splat!* – a wad of spit landed on my shoulder.

I was shocked and horrified. When I looked up the stairwell, two floors up stood one of the school's most notorious bad boys, laughing and pointing at me. I was instantly furious. It was a rage that shut out all other experience and thought. I charged up the stairs faster than I thought I could, grabbed him by the front of his shirt, and pushed him against the wall.

There was absolute silence as everyone was so shocked that I was standing up against the school bully. I screamed at him, "So you think spitting on someone is funny? Well, laugh at this!" and I spat on the front of his shirt. Then I turned around and walked slowly down the stairs. With each step, my legs felt more rubbery. I listened for footsteps coming down behind me, afraid that he would come out of his shock and beat me to a pulp.

As I got back to my place in line, the place erupted, and my heart started pounding like crazy. Those footsteps never came, and the bully treated me with a little more respect after that incident.

There were several other incidents in my life where that strong, sure personality came out and took over the situation. As I got older and survived both the Marine Corps and Viet Nam, that person was more and more in charge of my life.

I came to realize that when people perceived me as a strong, grounded person, there were fewer and fewer moments when I had to let my frustration out in a negative, uncontrolled way.

No one believes me now when I say I was shy as a young boy.

Life's Lessons

We never stop learning
whether we choose to or not.

Karma Might Get You

Watching people is one of my favorite pastimes. A friend and I had tickets for an evening concert. To get a good parking place, we went to the venue early. Since there was a shopping mall across the street from the arena, we decided to hang out there until show time. We had a nice meal, and then found some comfortable chairs to sit in and watch people go by.

We were enjoying the great variety of hairstyles and clothing, when I noticed a woman coming down the wide walkway. I nudged my friend and said, "Here comes someone who hasn't figured out that she has outgrown that type of dress."

She was wearing a stretchy strapless dress. On a naturally perky younger woman or one wearing an appropriate strapless bra, it would have looked attractive. This middle-aged woman had neither, so her breasts looked like two flat pieces of meat with a fold in between rather than cleavage.

The stretch material also accentuated her ample butt. As she passed by us, I thought of a quote I had heard years ago, "like two hogs fighting in a sack." We had to stifle our laughter.

In the next hour, she wandered by at least three times. On one of the closer passes, I noticed that she had a large, fleshy, pink mole on the front side of her shoulder. I pointed it out to my buddy, and he asked me, "What is that thing?"

Jokingly, I said, It looks like an extra nipple!" That time we couldn't hold our laughter in. We turned towards each other to make people think that one of us had told a great joke. A short time after she had passed by, I saw a young guy with a t-shirt that said, "Karma will get you."

I was sobered by that message and told my friend that I felt guilty for making fun of the woman, and that she was probably a very nice person who just didn't have friends to tell her how she should dress. My friend just gave me one of those looks.

The time to go to the concert came and we went across the street and found our seats. Just as we were settling in, we saw the same woman come up the stairs next to our seats. For a moment, I panicked because the seat beside me was not yet filled. I was afraid that she would have the seat beside me, and that I would have to try to ignore that 'extra nipple' all through the concert.

Luckily, she walked on by and went to the next section where she found her seat. I breathed a long sigh of relief, and my buddy turned to me and said, "Dude, it's a good thing you said something nice about her."

I just shook my head and said, "Yeah, karma can be a bitch."

Lessons From Our Pets

My family never had pets, so when I got married and my new husband said, "Let's get a dog," I was a little apprehensive. We ended up getting a beautiful Irish Setter puppy.

He was everything I had feared. He chewed everything; he messed in the house; he barked at everything that moved; in short, he was driving me crazy!

Then just after his first year with us, someone stole him from our back yard. We were heartbroken. I couldn't believe that I missed him so much. I had thought that I didn't like him, but he had wormed his way into my heart.

My husband worked in an office about a mile from our house, and he liked to walk to and from work to keep in shape. When it was raining, he would call and ask me to pick him up.

One rainy day, I picked him up and he had a box with him. I thought it was some work he was bringing home as he sometimes did that. Suddenly, a sound came from the box. He had a cute, little, black, curly-haired puppy in that box!

He told me it was called a cockapoo, but I didn't care as I had already fallen in love with her pretty face. When we got home, he told me a co-worker had bought her for his son, but it turned out he was allergic, so he had to find her a new home.

We were lucky to get her. My husband told me that her first owner, the little boy, had already given her a name–"Killer." In spite of the horrible name, she was everything the other dog had not been. She was intelligent, frisky, funny, easily trained and very affectionate. She became a member of the family immediately.

She was with us for 13 years. Our back yard was enclosed by a concrete wall. The neighbor's cat used to love to sit on the wall in the sun. When she was done with her nap, she would stretch and meow.

That was Killer's cue. He would jump up, race out the dog door and run over and bark at the cat. The cat would slowly walk along the fence while Killer jumped and barked, walking along in the yard below her. They went through the same exercise day after day for years.

Killer developed some health problems as she got older, and eventually, the vet told us we should put her down as she was in constant pain. We tearfully followed the vet's advice. We were devastated. The house seemed so empty.

The neighbor's cat began prowling the fence, yowling for hours. One day when I came home from shopping, the cat was in the front yard. When I opened the door carrying my two bags of groceries, she scooted in the house right under my feet.

She proceeded to investigate the whole house going room to room, and then she raced out the dog door, and after that, we never saw her on the back fence again.

All this time, we thought Killer and the cat were enemies, but in fact, they were friends who met every day to just greet each other. I learned that real friendships can grow even with someone very different from yourself.

Forever Blowing Bubbles

I have been attending an exercise class for seniors twice a week for several years. There are both men and women in the class. We talk, share, and laugh with each other as the woman on the video tells us what to do. We start sitting in a chair, but the second part of the program we do standing up.

As I stood up to get ready for the second part, I passed gas. "Oh, my," I said blushing, "Please excuse me for tooting."

A lady nearby said, "Don't worry about it. I do it all the time."

Suddenly, everyone seemed to have something to say about this problem.

Another woman said, "It wouldn't be so bad if I didn't do it in public so often. It's embarrassing when I'm in the checkout line. Some people stare and others laugh, but at least they don't crowd me."

"My granny always called it blowing bubbles. She would often start singing that song 'I'm Forever Blowing Bubbles.'"

A man who had heard this exchange said, "Oh, for God's sake. Call it what it is. It's a fart. And I don't care what anybody says, farts are funny."

Another guy piped up, "If I'm outside, I just call it my personal leaf blower."

One woman snorted and said, "Oh, you men! So typical–you make everything disgusting."

"Now wait a minute. You ladies are the one making it disgusting. It's a perfectly normal product of digestion. It is unhealthy **not** to fart."

One of the older ladies whom we all admired for her poise and dignity spoke up. "Girls, the men are right. Everyone farts and it is often funny. When my father farted, he always acted surprised and said that the frogs in the lake seemed to be getting hoarse."

"Let me tell you my story. I was interviewing for a job, and I could tell by the boss's reaction that I was going to get the job. But as he walked me to the door of his office, I tooted with every step."

"Did you get the job?"

"No! But I met that same guy about six months later. He came up to me at a job fair and asked me if I had ever applied for a job at his former company."

"I said vaguely that I thought I might have."

Then he started chuckling and asked, "Aren't you the lady that farted all the way to the door?"

I was shocked and was blushing horribly when he told me how much he had admired the matter-of-fact way I had handled the situation. I managed to get out a quiet "Thank you.'" Then he asked me to have dinner with him.

"Over dinner, he told me his former company was going through a restructuring at that time, and that the job I had interviewed for had just disappeared. He had also been phased out."

" A year later we were married. We were together for 47 years – and all because of a memorably noisy exit."

Just a Small Mistake

I live in a community for seniors. We look out for each other and socialize together. We often sit around and share our memories. Some of these stories make us laugh and laughing is good for our mental and physical health. They also jog our memory. Memory is one of the things that starts fading as we get older. It is frustrating, but we deal with it.

We often share meals. So that none of us have to do a lot of cooking, we have a potluck dinner. Sometimes, the whole community gets together on holidays. There are 70+ us, and although not everyone comes, it is great fun to taste all the many, many different dishes.

I filled up my plate and sat down with some friends. Everything was great. Some of the dishes I recognized, but there was one that I had never had before. I asked the people at my table if they knew who had brought that dish. Someone said that she thought Margaret, who was sitting at the next table, had brought it.

I yelled over at Margaret. "I love this new dish. What is it?"

She looked confused. I tried to describe it, and she finally got up and came over to see what I was talking about.

At first, she said, "I didn't bring that," but one of her neighbors, who was at my table, told her that she had walked over to the clubhouse with her, and that was the dish she was carrying.

Finally, Margaret turned back, grabbed her own spoon, and tasted it. Then she stirred it and tasted it again. She got a strange look on her face, and then she burst out laughing. She laughed so loud and long that she drew the attention of most of the people at the dinner.

"Oh My God!" she said when she could finally breathe. It's my tuna casserole, but I forgot to put in the tuna!

"Get Thee to a Nunnery" (Shakespeare)

My family did not understand me, and I had to get away. They were very religious, so at sixteen, I convinced them (with a lot of acting) that I had the 'calling' and wanted to be a nun. I was interviewed and accepted.

I stayed two years until I was eighteen and could legally remove myself from the convent and my family. The following is a slice of life in the convent which the mother superior expressly told me not to talk about.

Morning dormitory prayers had just finished when I heard Mary Ann open her door. I could never finish my morning ablutions as quickly as she did. After the bed had been made, we took our basins to the bathroom to empty, rinse, and dry them. We arranged the glass inside the basin and hung the folded hand towel on the side rail. All this was done with heads bowed and eyes cast down.

The last thing was to grab our long black socks from the previous day and take them to the basement where we stuffed them into our personally numbered pigeonhole. The socks would wait there until we finished morning mass and meditation.

After that, in the 'Great Silence,' we sedately went to pick up our socks. Then on to the laundry room, where we politely took turns washing our socks with brown soap. We then went out and hung them on the clothesline. Then it was off to breakfast to listen to the spiritual readings for the morning.

The Postulate Mistress would break the Great Silence and tell us when we were to retrieve our socks. It wasn't the same time every day. It depended on the weather, so it could be after noon prayers, after lunch, before afternoon classes, returning from our afternoon rosary walk, after making the stations of the cross at the cemetery, or while passing the grotto finishing our rosary. If the sisters needed the laundry, we would have an earlier sock schedule perhaps mid-morning.

In the evening after study hall and dinner, we had some time to darn our socks. Then already in the Great Silence again, we picked up our socks and returned to our rooms. The clean socks went on the back of the chair while the dirty socks from the day went beneath the seat.

Early on I came to realize that the long black socks were the only part of our daily routine that refused to be controlled. The times of the other daily routine never changed, but the time when we could recover our socks from the clothesline was different almost every day due to weather, changes in our schedule, etc.

I felt a deep connection to those socks, as I, too, was different and didn't want to be constricted by family or society. Two years of constriction in the convent bought me my freedom.

An Unexpected Lesson

After I graduated from high school, I went to Washington, D.C., with a business card from my dad in my pocket. It was my first summer away from home, and I wanted to learn how politics and government worked.

I volunteered to work for my congressman as a clerk typist in the Department of the Interior. I also wanted to participate in the Poor People's Campaign.

I showed up on my first day only to realize that I could not pass the civil service typing test. Then surprisingly, my boss found someone to take the test for me and asked me to lie on the form in order to qualify for the job.

I worked for political campaigns in the evening in the bowels of the Senate building, and I was shocked to find out that it was a machine that signed the letters from my congressman. There were other things going on that I didn't really understand, but I got the impression that they weren't to be asked about.

On the weekends, I marched for the Poor People's Campaign to end hunger in America, and to honor Martin Luther King, who had been shot several months earlier. It was inspiring to be a part of it, but my supervisor told me not to talk about it at work. Several of the photographs I took are now on file with the National Park Service showing life at Resurrection City, where many volunteers lived.

With time and experience, my typing speed and accuracy improved, making me feel like a somewhat competent civil servant. However, I came to recognize that so much of what I did was bureaucracy that accomplished nothing.

Lying in the grass on the National Mall and watching the Fourth of July fireworks, I thought how lucky I was to be watching the most spectacular show in the world in our nation's capital.

I took a trip to New York City to see the United Nations before going home. I took the tour but wasn't able to talk to anyone who worked there. Still, I could smell the familiar, stale smell of bureaucracy there too.

Soon I was flying home and getting ready to attend college in Los Angeles. I majored in diplomacy and world affairs even though I had definitely lost my political innocence that summer.

One Thing Led to Another

It all started when a friend gave me an incredible artistic wall hanging that she had made. I had admired it since I first saw it, and since she was moving and had to downsize, she gave it to me.

I was overwhelmed and grateful, but when I got it home, I realized that I didn't have an empty space on any wall that would do it justice. When she gave it to me, she had also told me that I would need to paint the wall it was going to hang on a specific color to bring out the subtleties of the work.

After a couple of weeks, I realized that I was going to have to redo an entire room to put up my new treasure. I had to sell a desk, two bookcases, and a hide-a-bed to empty the room. Then I got the right color and painted the room.

The morning after I finished painting, I woke up and walked into the room to get something out of the closet and had one of those disconcerting 'the world is upside down' moments. The room seemed to have grown bigger somehow.

That was how it started. My whole apartment somehow looked different to me. I came face to face with all the stuff that I had packed away in closets and drawers. I took a deep breath and started to go through everything and purge, purge, purge!

It took a lot of time and energy, but it was liberating. All those memories gave me a real glimpse into my life in my earlier years. I learned that I am so much more now than I was then.

Of course, there are some things that I saved because they have a lasting meaning to me. Most of the things that I had saved for some reason were just taking up space, both physical and emotional, and had lost all meaning to me. I threw away boxes and bags of things or took them to one of the thrift stores.

Getting rid of all this stuff was amazingly freeing. It was like having years of psychiatric sessions. I realized that much of the stuff was connected to the ways I had tried to please people. I had spent way too much time worrying about what other people thought of me and my work.

It's not that you shouldn't please others, but when you repress a part of yourself in order to make others happy or comfortable, you are hurting yourself. I see now that many people do this for so long that they don't even know their real selves anymore.

If people can't love you for your real self, they don't love you at all. I am trying to be more authentic with myself and others. It's not easy and some of my acquaintances are uncomfortable with the 'new' me.

On the other hand, I have nothing to lose except boxes, bags, papers, and junk taking up space in my apartment, in my computer, and in my mind.

All this was going on while the new furniture I bought was being delivered and installed into the new bedroom. It changed the whole room, and I finally had a place to sit and stare at my new wall hanging.

Who to Trust?

Kids can be cruel to each other. Some of us have been on the receiving end of bullies, some have been the bullies, and some have just looked on and thanked God that they weren't being picked on.

Maybe that is just the way humans interact naturally, I don't know. But what I learned growing up is that adults are really not that different. They just have better ways and more words to hide their bullying, prejudices, and stupidity.

The first event that made me re-evaluate adults happened when I was ten or eleven. My family were members of a fairly conservative church. My Sunday school teacher was giving us a special lesson just before Easter. He was driving home the point that Jesus died for our sins. I understood that, but when he said that if you didn't know Jesus, you went to hell, I knew that he was wrong.

I reminded him that some people had never had a chance to learn about Jesus through no fault of their own like the American Indians, but he insisted they all went to hell. I then asked about the people who had lived a good life even though they had never heard of the Ten Commandments, and he said they also went to hell.

I shut up because I had already learned by that time that a kid could never win an argument with an adult, but I knew from a source deep within me that he was wrong. This was the first time that I had felt that internal voice that spoke with such absolute authority. Over the course of my life, I was to hear that voice a number of times and learn to trust what it said.

Later in high school, the coach noticed me shooting baskets in PE class, and asked me to try out for the basketball team. I practiced all summer in my back yard. I was a little short and small compared to the others, but I could shoot better than most of them.

The problem was that basketball isn't all shooting. You have to move the ball up and down the court and cooperate with your teammates. I wasn't good at that part of the game, but I made the team.

When the first away game came, there wasn't enough room on the bus for everyone, so the coach told me that my friend Gary would go this time, and I would get to go the next time.

When the next time came, I was again told I couldn't go with the team. I reminded the coach of what he had promised me the last time, but he said I must have misunderstood.

My friend Gary stood up for me and said, "No, coach. That is what you said." He immediately kicked both of us off the team. Not only was I crushed, but Gary wouldn't talk to me for weeks.

When I became a teacher and then later a teacher trainer, I came to the realization that some people only become teachers to have a platform where their profession allows them to get away with acting like bullies and dictators.

It's a little harder for adults to fool other adults, but they still try. If they have some sort of position that allows them some status, they are more likely to succeed in their lies. Sounds a lot like politicians at all levels, doesn't it?

Trust yourself! Decide what's true for yourself, and you'll never be a victim!

Things Not Talked About

I teach an Introduction to American Culture class for newly arrived international students.   I use a series of models to illustrate various aspects of culture. An iceberg represents that the most important part of culture – values – are invisible.

Another of the models I use to illustrate culture is a 'can of worms.' When I was a kid, we would dig up worms to use for bait to go fishing. Worms in a can become so intertwined that it is hard to pull out just one of them. Culture is like that, hard to define due to the interconnectedness of many factors.

This class is supposed to emphasize the differences in academic procedures and policies to help them do well in their US college classes. The truth is that academic culture is so inter-connected to many other cultural factors, that I end up talking about many other aspects of American culture.

What I love about teaching is that I learn something from my students almost every day. In this class especially, I get to see my own culture through the eyes of someone outside my culture.

Because of my lifetime of working with international students in the area of cultural pluralism, I don't see one set of ideas, values, and behaviors as better or worse than any others. I only see these factors as different and interesting. The students' observations of American culture are often eye opening to me. At times, they ask me "Why?" and I have no answer. We never think to deeply about our own culture; we just live it.

The last few years have been challenging for me as several friends have passed away. Some of them have been younger than I am, and that certainly changed my attitudes and priorities.

The impending death of a dear friend was shaking me to the core and was affecting everything I did including teaching classes, so I shared with my students what was happening in my life. The class wanted to talk and read about the American approach to dying.

Americans make such a production out of death. Funerals are more elaborate and expensive than ever before. So many people that have never even known the deceased are involved while the family has little to do but sit and grieve–and pay!

I can remember when my great grandmother died. When we went back to my grandfather's farm after the funeral, he changed out of his good clothes and started out the door. My mother asked him where he was going, and he said, "to milk the cows, of course."

Then my grandmother got up and told him to wait until she changed. My mom quickly said that she would go to do the milking as grandma might like a little more time to grieve the death of her mother, but grandma said, "you would just scare the cows."

In the old days, life went on almost immediately after death and burial. This shows how culture changes over time. A few years ago, I had to make the arrangements for a friend who had passed away and was shocked when the funeral home told me that they were booked up for the next 2 weeks!

Why are people so afraid of death? It is a natural part of our life cycle and nothing we can do will alter that. I was shocked when my uncle and father, both of whom were strongly religious, found little or no comfort in their faith at the end of their lives. They both were mad at God for letting them suffer painfully in their last days. There are other cultures who think that the pain is there to teach us to surrender to the absolute and leave all the attachments of this world behind.

What has medical science done to the process of dying? People used to just die when the time came. Now families try to keep their loved ones around as long as possible no matter what it takes or how much it costs.

Can't they see that is selfish? It has little or nothing to do with the person dying. It is just for those who will be left behind.

I think we need to have better education about death and dying, but that is the problem – no one wants to talk about it – parents or teachers. Besides, death has become big business for doctors and undertakers.

It's a part of American culture that I can't explain very well when my students ask me why?

Party Hearty

When you are a grad student, every weekend is an excuse for a party. I can't remember if it was Halloween or Mardi Gras or what, but for this party we were supposed to dress in costume. I wasn't up to getting a costume together, so I had decided not to go.

My friend called and announced that my absence was unacceptable and demanded that I appear. When I explained that I didn't have a costume, she said to come anyway, and she would 'costume' me there. I had no other excuse, so I wandered over to her house, which was nearby.

Four people lived in the house, three women and one man. They were studying different fields but got along well. I knew them all pretty well as I had been over there a number of times. The guy was from Sweden and was a bit unusual at times.

I came in through the back door and got myself a beer. There were a number of people there and the booze was flowing freely. Some people were in full costume and others just wore masks. It was some minutes before my friend found me mixing with the other guests.

She immediately dragged me into her bedroom where she proceeded to give me a big floppy sun hat and put some black makeup around my eyes. As a final touch she put some black lipstick on me. With my aloha shirt and shorts, I looked like some sort of ghoul headed for the beach.

Sometime later, I needed to go to the bathroom, but found the bathroom was not only occupied, but there was a line waiting outside the door. My friend walked by and whispered that I could go upstairs to Lars' bathroom. His room was the master bedroom, so it had a private bathroom.

I realized then that I hadn't seen him in the throng of party guests. I asked where he was. She said that she hadn't seen him since earlier when he had said something about getting ready.

I went upstairs to Lars' room. I opened the door and went in. The bathroom door was ajar, so thinking that Lars was not around, I went in and flipped on the light.

I walked over to the commode and had started to pee when the shower curtain was slowly pulled back. I was shocked to see Lars lying in the tub. He had apparently fallen asleep while taking a bath. I hardly recognized him as he had cut off his longish blonde hair and shaved his head.

As I was staring at him, he was staring at me. "Oh, you're circumcised," he observed, which made me feel very vulnerable. Apparently, my emotions were easily read on my face because he suddenly stood up and said, "I'm not, but then most Europeans aren't."

As he unabashedly showed me his penis, I was shocked to realize that he had no pubic hair either. He had shaved that too! Again, he must have seen the shocked expression on my face because he said, "I'm glad you're here because you can help me finish the job."

"What?" I said completely confused.

"I need you to shave my backside. I can't have any body hair as I am going as a baby tonight."

He then produced a bottle of Swedish vodka, poured me a glass, and offered a toast which we drank down in one gulp. Then he handed me a razor and turned his back to me.

What could I do but start shaving him? I soon realized that I would have to shave his butt and the backs of his legs. It was a little more intimate than most guys would have felt comfortable with, but the fact that I was feeling suddenly high from the beer and his vodka, and that he also seemed pretty smashed made it possible for me to finish the job he had started.

After he had rinsed off, he fashioned a diaper out of a dish towel, pinned it with big safety pins, and after another couple of toasts with the good Swedish vodka, led the way downstairs.

I was glad that I had come as it turned out to be a great party after all. We danced, drank, and talked until the wee hours of the morning. I got hungry towards the end of the night when most of the guests had already gone. I asked my friend if I could have one of the bananas on the table in the kitchen. We were all pretty drunk by that time.

She grabbed a banana and started to hand it to me, but then she disappeared onto the back porch. She quickly returned and attached the banana to my fly with a clothes pin! We all laughed.

About that time 'baby' Lars came into the kitchen. He laughed, but said, "Wait!" He went to the silverware drawer and got a knife and cut off the end of the banana, and said, "There, now that's more realistic."

It was all great fun at the time, but the next day we all suffered mightily from our carousing. After a few more really bad grad-school hangovers, I gave up drinking altogether.

Tonight's 'Factoid' Is...

I live in a lovely complex with mostly retired people. We have a lovely open area between buildings where we have many outdoor chairs and a table. On evenings when the weather allows, we meet and have wide-ranging conversations.

One evening, one of the residents introduced a new piece of information that she had heard on a nature show on PBS. She called her new information a 'Factoid.' She told us that the most interesting information was that birds didn't have sphincters.

Some of our members are highly educated, but some are not. All are treated equally, but sometimes the difference becomes more obvious.

One of the ladies asked, "What's a sphincter?"

As with all groups, we have different personalities, so one of the 'wild cards' of the group said very directly, "It's an asshole."

The abruptness of the message and the very directness of the answer caused the group to break down in raucous laughter.

Then someone remarked, "That must be why they crap on everything–even people when they are flying overhead."

The answer to that was, "So you don't think it's personal?"

"What have I ever done to a bird?" came the reply.

We all enjoy the witty repartee on these evenings, but I went away a little confused and doubtful. I kept thinking about how all birds lay eggs.

A few days later, I remembered to look up this 'factoid' on the computer. On a scientific website, I found that although birds don't have the same musculature that mammals have, which is called a sphincter, they do have some muscles which help to control their egg laying.

I copied the information and read it the next time the group met. The information included the scientific word 'cloaca' which was used instead of the word sphincter.

When I finished reading, the predictable question followed, "What's a cloaca?"

Again, came the answer, "It's another word for asshole."

"Well, I don't need to know all those fancy words for assholes. As long as mine still works, that's all I care about."

That brought the house down, and we laughed heartily for at least 5 minutes. When we settled down, someone said, "Well, that really caused my sphincter to contract."

The laughter went on and on.

I wonder what the next 'factoid' will bring.

New Places

New Friends

Travel opens our lives up
to new cultures and people
and interesting adventures.

A Slip of the Tongue

It's hard to learn a new language when you are an adult, but there I was in Japan, trying to learn Japanese. One of the services the language school provided was homestay placement. They found me a room near the school. The landlady was nice but spoke no English. I assumed that this was to make me learn the language quickly.

I thought I was doing fairly well and tried to use Japanese as often as I could. I bought a really good dictionary and kept a notebook of new words, paying special attention to those words that didn't come up in my classes.

When June came, it started raining. My teacher explained that Japan had a rainy season that sometimes lasted months (or at least it seemed like it!). I had never experienced anything like that. Everything was wet all the time. It was kind of a pain.

One day, when I opened the closet in my room, I noticed that the back wall had changed color. Upon closer inspection, I discovered that the wall was wet and covered with some sort of mildew. I immediately went to my dictionary. It took some time, but I found a word that I thought described the stuff–"kabi." I had already learned the word for closet–"oshiro"–in one of the class dialogues.

Then I went to the landlady and tried to explain the situation.

I delivered the Japanese sentence that I had written out and practiced in my room, but she just stared at me. I carefully repeated the sentence again, but she just frowned.

She finally answered me, but it took some time for me to understand what she said. Using my dictionary, I finally figured out that she was asking me if I needed to see a doctor. I was confused, so through some broken Japanese and sign language, I got her to come to my room so I could show her the problem.

She took one look and burst out laughing. She could hardly contain herself. Finally, when she could talk, she pointed to the closet and said, "Oshiro." I nodded and agreed. She then blushed and pointed at my rear end and said, "Oshiri."

It was my turn to blush and then laugh when I realized that due to a small mistake in pronunciation, I had told her that I had mildew in my ass!

No wonder she asked if I needed a doctor.

Proper English

One of my dearest friends is British but has lived in America for many years. She still has her accent, so everyone knows where she came from. Funnily enough, her family in England thinks that she has an American accent!

One of the most interesting things in our time together has been when we misunderstood each other even though we both speak English, but maybe not the same kind of English.

The first time this became obvious was when we were going to a meeting. Since there was limited parking at the meeting site, she thought there was no reason for us both to drive, and she had the nicer car. She called me and said, "I'll just swing by and knock you up." I was stunned for a moment and then said, "I'd like to see you try that." Then I broke down laughing.

I remember another time when her mother was visiting from England. She made a fantastic dinner for her mother and had invited friends to meet her. The first course was vichyssoise, a French, cold potato soup. I loved it and wanted to learn how to make it.

After dinner, when she and her mother were doing dishes in the kitchen, I found a pen and paper and asked her to tell me how to make this delicious soup.

The first thing she said in her very proper high-class accent was, "First, you have to take a leek." That was it, I lost it and laughed so hard I could hardly breathe!

Her mother turned around from the sink and asked her very seriously if I was all right. She explained to her mother that the phrase 'take a leak' had a different meaning to people in the US.

I'll never forget her mother shaking her head and saying, "Oh, these Americans!"

One day my friend was driving down the street near her home when smoke started coming out from under the hood of her car. She pulled into the first filling station she saw and jumped out of the car.

A young man came out of the station, and in a panic, she pointed and said, "There's a fire in the bonnet!" He was totally confused by that but asked if she had a fire extinguisher.

She pointed to the back of the car and said, "It's in the boot!"

Even though she had lived in the US for years, in a time of emergency, she could only use the vocabulary she had learned as a young girl in England–(bonnet = hood, boot = trunk).

Her mother and other family members visited several times, and I was invited to visit them in England. There were a few misunderstandings while I was there. One time when I was staying with her mother, I called her 'Mum' as the family did, but she let me know that Brits were not so familiar, and that I was to call her by her given name, Helen.

Helen made dinner one night and asked if I liked it. I said that it was quite good. She didn't respond the way I thought she would but didn't think much of it. The next day at lunch, I said, "Let's eat up the rest of what we had for dinner last night."

She looked at me, blinked, and said, "I thought you didn't like it."

"No," I said, "It was really good. Why did you think I didn't like it?" Then she explained to me that the word 'quite' has a mostly negative meaning in British English. Who knew?

One day, Helen said that she wanted me to experience a traditional pub lunch. As we left her flat (not apartment), I headed for her car, but she said, "It's only a short walk to get there."

Thirty minutes later, I was huffing and puffing as we got to the pub. I said, "Is that your idea of a short walk?" She laughed and said, "Oh, that's right. I've been told that you Americans never walk anywhere. Brits love walking. We do walking tours all over the countryside."

Once when I was with my friend's sister and family, some plans for a family party had to be changed at the last minute due to a car problem. She turned to me and said, "Well, that's gone tits up!" Seeing the look on my face, she said, "I guess I should have said, It's gone pear-shaped." That didn't make sense to me either.

I was sort of stunned by that expression and when I told my British friend about it, she said, "When I first came to the US, I was appalled by Americans saying, 'That really pisses me off.' In England that would be a shocking thing to say.

I visited my friend's sister who had two boys while I was in England. After dinner, they were doing homework at the kitchen table when the younger (age 11) asked the older (age 15) for a rubber. I quickly glanced up at the parents wondering what they were going to say, but they went on reading the newspaper. I got up and wandered into the kitchen to see what was going on. I soon put two and two together and figured out that for Brits, a rubber is an eraser. Whew!

After visiting Helen and the family several times, I knew my way around the town where they lived. While standing on a corner waiting for the light to change, a little old lady pulled on my sleeve and asked me if I knew where the grocery store was. I did and told her that it was very easy to get there. After I had finished telling her the directions, she looked up at me and said, "You're not from around here, are you?" in a sort of dismissive tone.

I guess it was my accent. She crossed the street, and promptly stopped a lady and asked her the same question she had asked me. The lady gave her exactly the same directions I had given her. As she started to walk off, she turned and frowned at me.

I guess I wasn't supposed to know anything about the locality as I was a foreigner.

My Santorini Encounter

As our cruise ship pulled into the pier at Santorini, one of the Greek islands on our tour, I realized that the city was on top of a big cliff. There were three choices to get up to the city: walk, ride a donkey or a take the tram.

My athletic son-in-law chose to walk, but my daughter and I rode the tram. At the top of the hill, he went off to see something he had read about in a brochure, but we decided to go shopping along the high street.

I was looking for some more appropriate clothes as it was quite hot in Greece at that time of the year. I saw something in a window that I wanted to check out, so we went into the small store.

We were the only ones in the store except for the beautiful lady behind the counter. We both were struck by how much she looked like the famous star Sophia Loren. She was gorgeous! We started to look around and then made conversation with her when she spoke to us in English.

As I was getting ready to pay for my new skirt, my daughter noticed a picture of the lady and a good-looking man. The lady explained, "This is me and my husband. I lost him last year. He was the town's doctor. He was wonderful and kind. Sometimes he accepted fish or vegetables as payment from those who could not afford his services."

Then tears began to well up in her eyes. We looked at each other, and my daughter suddenly asked her if she would like to pray together. She said, "Oh, please." The prayer was short, and I don't remember much about it. We hugged and left the shop.

My daughter and I still speak of Santorini's lovely Sophia Loren and the magic of our meeting.

A Life-Changing Trip

After my college graduation in 1972, I went to Japan out of curiosity, and when I landed at the Haneda Airport in Tokyo, I looked around and asked myself, "What have I done?" because none of the signs were in English, and I did not know Japanese.

After spending a week in Tokyo, I needed to leave because there were just too many people living so close together. Everyone was on the trains at the same time, making me feel lost and like a sardine.

I remembered a Japanese friend from college had told me that I would be welcome to visit his family in Kyoto. So, I took the train and went to visit his family, and I met his parents, the Kanos.

Mama-san and Papa-san welcomed me with open arms and took me in like a second son, introducing me to neighbors and making me feel special even though I didn't speak any Japanese.

One night I was invited to visit their restaurant, Kano Sushi, located just down the street. Businessmen would stop by in the evening, and they all wanted to practice spoken English. I was happy to give free English lessons to everyone.

Kano Sushi soon became even more popular. Papa-san gave me free sushi and sake. Every night I would go and enjoy meeting new friends. My love for Japan was forever solidified.

I enrolled in the Kyoto Language School to learn some Japanese and made some international friends who were also studying there. We got together for Thanksgiving dinner. It was not exactly the same, eating chicken instead of turkey, but we stuffed ourselves like we would have done back home.

Later, I met a woman who wanted me to teach an English class to the children in her village. They called me Mr. Tom, and I would ride the train to her home in the country and teach English to about twenty Japanese children and then ride the train back to where I was staying.

I got tired of riding the train and moved to the village. I lived by myself, and that time alone made me feel like I was in a monastery. It gave me time to think about my life, and what I wanted to do with my future.

After a year, the local police came to visit the Kano's. I was occasionally visiting their restaurant, and they told me that I had overextended my tourist visa. They said I was required to visit the local police station and plead guilty.

I was scared. During the interview, they asked me questions about my family and told me that I had shamed my family by my unlawful behavior. I mumbled a traditional formal "I am sorry," and they told me to leave the country within a week.

I was soon on an airplane headed back home full of wonderful memories and experiences, and gratitude to the Kano family and my young English students for what was the beginning of my love affair with Japan.

A Random Meeting

Mozart's 250th birthday was celebrated in Austria in 2006. There were men and boys dressed as Mozart everywhere, selling anything that they could somehow connect with Mozart. My favorite was a kind of candy they called Mozart's Chocolate Balls!

I visited the Mozart Museum in Salzburg, and then went on to Vienna. I saw an ad for a Mozart string quartet concert, to be held in one of the rooms that Mozart had used when he lived in Vienna.

It was in a rather small room with seating for only about 30 people. The weather had turned hot, and there were very few places in Austria (or most parts of Europe for that matter) that had air conditioning.

With so many people crammed together in a small room, the heat soon became unbearable. We were all, even the musicians, literally dripping with sweat. After about fifteen minutes, the violinist turned to the audience, apologized, and said that they had to take a break due to the heat.

As we filed out of the stifling room, we felt an almost unnoticeable breeze, and I said to myself under my breath, "Well, at least it is a little cooler out here." The man behind me who had been sitting next to me inside suddenly said, "Oh, you're American." We began a conversation and soon found out that we were both language teachers.

He told me he had been born in Vienna but had lived and worked in the US for more than 40 years. He owns an apartment in Vienna and comes back to Austria for several weeks every year.

We were eventually called back into the room, and the musicians finished the concert, which was actually very good, especially considering the conditions.

After the concert, my new friend insisted I accompany him to a special ice cream shop. According to him, ice cream is one thing the Austrians do very well. He was right, of course; it was fantastic. We exchanged email addresses and promised to keep in touch, and we did.

Over time, we found we had the same outlook on life. He kept inviting me to come and stay with him in his apartment in Vienna. His wife, who is originally from Brazil, and his grown daughter had been to Vienna with him several times but didn't share his love for the city, so most years he went alone.

For several years, I didn't make it back to Vienna, but a few years later, I went and stayed with him. I had some apprehension as to whether it would be a comfortable visit or not. After all, we had only spent a couple of hours together and exchanged emails for several years.

It turned out to be a great experience. We talked about anything and everything. At one point he laughed and said that our political views were surprisingly similar. I have stayed with him several times and now try to make sure that I stop by Vienna whenever we're both in Europe, even if it is only for a few days.

If I hadn't gone to the concert, and muttered to myself in English, and if he hadn't spoken to me, I would have missed many great experiences with a very good friend. That unexpected moment at a concert in Vienna changed my life for the better.

Herr Haar Hier?

The second time I was in Europe, I spent some months studying in Switzerland. Looking in the mirror one morning, I realized that I would probably need a haircut before I went back to the U.S. I had noticed that there was not the separation between beauty shops for women and barber shops for men like we have in the States. Every hair salon was for both men and women.

I walked by the same salon almost every day while I was staying in the city where I was studying. The shop had a big window in front, and I couldn't help but notice the gentleman who worked there cutting hair every day. One day as I came by, he was outside the shop smoking.

He greeted me in Swiss German, and although my German wasn't too good, I knew how to answer. He immediately smiled and said in English, "Oh, you are an American." So much for my accent! We talked for a short while, and he said, "Come by when you need a cut." I thanked him and went on.

Since I was attending classes, I was pretty busy most days. Finally, I had a day with some extra time, so I decided to go visit my new acquaintance and get a haircut.

You can imagine my surprise when I opened the door and the barber wasn't there. Instead, there was a very attractive young lady. I wasn't sure if she worked there as she was reading a magazine and only looked up as I came in.

I looked around and struggled to find the German words to ask about the gentleman who usually worked there. It came out "Herr Haar hier?" Which meant, "Mr. Hair here?" She gave me a strange look, and then said something which I didn't understand.

I just stood there with my mouth hanging open, so she repeated what she had said before, and this time I recognized that it was French, but I didn't speak enough French to know what she said.

Finally, she gestured towards the chair. I had to make up my mind quickly. Was I going to turn and leave, or let her cut my hair? I was frozen in place, and before I could make my own decision, she took my elbow and guided me into the chair.

As I sat down, I began to wonder how I could tell her what I wanted. Then I realized that I knew the word for little in French – 'petite.' With much gesturing, I conveyed that I just wanted a little taken off – a trim.

As I looked into the mirror, she slapped the back of my head with a comb, and as a lock of hair flew up above my head, she cut most of it off! I was stunned. What was she doing? While I was trying to understand, lock after lock was falling to the floor. I finally just closed my eyes.

When she was finished, I had a haircut like nothing I had ever had before. It wasn't what I wanted, but it wasn't bad either. I guessed that it was a European style. She then wrote down the amount, and I paid and left.

All my friends seemed to like my new cut, and one interesting result of this haircut was that when I was out and about in the city, people now seemed to think I was German, not American. It did help me improve my German faster as most people spoke to me in German.

In short, I was able to work on expanding my vocabulary and correct my American accent, thanks to an accidental haircut.

Mi Amiga

It was my first Spanish class. I had chosen a section with a teacher who had a Spanish-sounding name – Sanchez. As the door opened, we all gasped. The teacher looked like she should be on her way to the hospital. She was so pregnant that she could hardly get through the door!

After dumping her hand-tooled leather briefcase on the desk, she turned and said, "As you can see, I won't be teaching this class the whole semester." At least that's what we finally figured out she said. She had a very strong accent. Then she opened the book and began lesson one – in Spanish!

Every day, the class was noticeably smaller. No one had ever been in a language class where the teacher never spoke a word of English. One of my classmates told me that he too had tried to get into another Spanish language section, but that they were all full.

The next class, the door opened, and at first, we thought a new student had been added to the class; but then she walked to the desk, took a paper out of her bag, and started calling names.

The new teacher was young, short, overweight, and wore her hair in two braids on each side of her head. She was blond and very light skinned – not Latina looking at all, but she spoke Spanish fluently.

Ms. Schmitz used a sort of rapid-fire type of questioning as we went through the lessons in class. Some students said that she had a 'Gestapo' style of teaching, but I sort of enjoyed it.

One day she announced that a famous Mexican poet was going to give a reading on campus, and that we could get extra credit if we attended. I jumped at the chance to get extra credit.

I went to the reading and searched the crowd so she would see me and give me the extra credit, and I finally found her on the floor in the back of the auditorium with a small baby on a blanket.

As she got out her grade book to log me in, I played with the baby. The baby and I were having a good time interacting when she finally noticed. I stayed with her and the baby during the reading. Although I didn't ask, she told me that she was an unmarried mother, and he was her son.

She also told me that her family was rather religious, so that made it doubly hard since she still lived with them. When I eventually became a regular in their lives, I must admit that it was awkward at times. I loved being with her and the baby, and eventually we became lovers.

We moved away from each other for schooling and better jobs, but we never lost touch. When she retired many years later, we went on a European trip together. She wanted to visit some of the famous European churches in Spain and Italy.

Our first stop was Santiago de Compostela. That's the church at the end of the famous trail from southern France to the northwest of Spain. This area is called Galicia, and the Spanish spoken there is influenced by Portuguese, which is spoken across the nearby border in northern Portugal.

I had studied Portuguese in grad school and had just come from a family trip to Portugal. I got along fairly well with the local dialect, while she had some problems since she had taught only pure Castilian Spanish for many years. Over dinner one evening, she made the snide comment that I handled the language fairly well for someone who only got a C- in her class.

Our next stop was Barcelona, all the way across Spain. The famous church there is the Familia Sagrada, which was designed by Gaudi. In Barcelona they speak another type of Spanish dialect called Catalan. I had visited Barcelona a number of times, so I got along fairly easily with the change in dialect.

Our last stop was Rome, and since Italian is fairly close to Spanish, she got along better there than I did with the language difference. After touring St. Peter's, I took her to my favorite restaurant in Rome.

After looking over the menu, she decided to order the four-cheese pizza. Since I had been to Italy a number of times, I started to explain about the pizza she was ordering, but she stopped me and said that she knew all about pizza.

When the food came, she looked at her plate and said, "What's that?"

"That is your four-cheese pizza," I replied.

"It looks like a giant cracker with melted cheese on it," she said.

"Exactly," I said, "I was trying to tell you that not all pizzas in Italy have tomato sauce on them."

"Oh," she said contritely, "Sorry for yelling at you."

"No problem. Eat up. I think you'll like it."

She ate every last crumb and pronounced it one of the best pizzas she had ever had.

She and I were dear friends for many years even though we didn't live near enough to be a regular part of each other's lives.

It was a lucky turn of events when Ms. Sanchez's water broke, and Ms. Schmitz took over her class.

Czech-Mate

In 1970, I was working at the US Mission to the United Nations in the beautiful city of Geneva, Switzerland. At the same time, my friend Kathy was working at the American Embassy in Prague. She invited me to come visit her. My mother's family was originally from Czechoslovakia, and I'd never been there, so I decided to go. I was busy organizing an international conference in Geneva, so I could only go for a long weekend.

Kathy not only worked at the embassy, but she was required to live in the building as well. Down in the basement, there was a commissary, so she literally didn't have to ever leave the embassy building. In fact, she had never even met any Czech people yet!

Visiting her wasn't easy since Czechoslovakia was Communist controlled at that time, so I had to apply for a government permit. Then I had to pay for a hotel (which the government chose) along with prepaying for meal vouchers. I was planning on staying in the embassy with Kathy, so I wasn't going to use the hotel, but I had to pay for the whole package anyway.

Her situation was oppressive. She suspected that her cleaning lady was a government spy, so she had no privacy to voice her thoughts or commit them to paper. If our conversations verged towards the political, she got very nervous. Kathy seemed depressed with her situation.

When I persuaded her to come with me to explore the city, I was shocked to learn that it was the first time she had gone out and about in Prague. We had a good time, although she seemed nervous at times and looked around a lot.

Kathy had to work part of that weekend, so I was on my own some of the time to wander the streets of pretty, old-world

Prague. People were always very friendly and helpful. Some tried to talk to me at the bus or tram stops. Unfortunately, as we went through the languages I knew-French, Portuguese and Greek, and the languages they knew-Czech, Slovakian, Russian and German, we couldn't come up with a common language. Only a few spoke English, so usually, we just had to give up.

One day I found myself near the hotel I was supposed to have stayed in, and I thought I should at least let them know that I wasn't going to stay there. When I showed them my vouchers, they were extremely upset that I had spent all that money and wasn't going to use any of the package. They suggested that I use the meal vouchers to invite a group of my friends for dinner there. These sweet, honest people kept insisting until I finally agreed to bring my friends for dinner.

On my last evening in Prague, Kathy brought along a friend, the son of the ambassador, and the three of us went to the little hotel for a nice local dinner. While we were eating, I noticed that there was only one other person in the restaurant. He was a large, rather severe-looking man sitting alone at a table nearby.

He sat there during our entire meal without ordering anything. I noticed that the waitstaff never approached him, and that they were noticeably less warm and friendly than when I had first met them. When we got up to leave, the big guy left as well.

By then, I knew what was going on, but I left Prague with a warm feeling from the sweetness and honesty of the Czech people who were so put upon and apparently constantly spied on.

To this day, I wonder if the big man was sent to spy on the hotel staff, Kathy, the Ambassador's son, or me.

Finding a True Friend

It was my fourth time to live and work in Japan, and this was the best job I had ever had considering the pay was much better, the position was much higher, and it included benefits like housing and free Japanese language classes.

I was on my way to the first session of the class. I found the building and saw a note telling all students to come to the seventh floor. I pushed the elevator button, and while I was waiting for it to come, several other people came in and stood behind me.

When the elevator arrived, we all were surprised to see how small it was. We all tried to crowd in as it had taken a rather long time to arrive, and no one wanted to be late to the first class.

Everyone was silent as the elevator started up, but I couldn't resist making some off-hand comment about the closeness. The guy beside me chuckled at my comment, but everyone else remained quiet. Later, that gentleman ended up in the same class with me.

We introduced ourselves, and I found out his name was Stefan, and that he was from Germany and was doing post graduate work at the university. Little did I know at that moment that he would become one of the best friends in my life.

We spent quite a bit of time together exploring what the area had to offer. We both had contacts from our daily interactions, and they took us to interesting places in the area.

Since we were spending quite a bit of time together, I felt compelled to explain to him that I was gay, and that others might think our relationship was more than just a friendship.

He was upset by my disclosure–not at me, but at other people for being so small-minded to even think such gossip. He told me that my sexuality was of no concern to him and didn't affect our friendship one way or the other. He was the first straight man in my life who completely accept me for who I was.

The first time we went to an *onsen* (a natural hot springs) in Japan, Stefan told me while undressing that he didn't want me to be shocked by the scars on his chest. He had been born with a congenital heart problem and had undergone a serious operation when he was 9 years old.

This was many years ago before the advent of all the modern methods of heart surgery, and the scars were actually pretty horrible. Going to *onsens* with friends became one of our favorite things to do on weekends, and there were always some people staring at his scars.

Later his wife joined him in Japan. She was from Switzerland. I helped her find a job teaching German and French at the local Berlitz school. We had a great time cooking together and getting to know other expats in the area.

We became very close while living in Japan, and later they visited me in the U.S. I visited them in Switzerland several times where Stefan was first a college professor, and later worked for a think tank headquartered in Zurich.

Several years after he had been working in Switzerland, he had to have more heart surgery. The operation went well although he had a few complications. When he was fully recovered, he went back to work.

Several years later, Stefan collapsed while doing some moderate, medically recommended exercise in the company health club. Immediately, other workers called for help, and he was rushed to the hospital. Unfortunately, he never came out of the coma and died eleven days later, leaving behind his wife and two young daughters.

I have maintained my connection with the family and have visited a number of times since Stefan left us. We are just getting to the point where we can talk about the good times we spent with Stefan.

Stefan was a very special man and meeting him in an elevator in Japan was one of my life's magic moments.

Is That English?

I lived and worked in Japan on several occasions. I was there to teach English to Japanese English teachers who knew English grammar but couldn't speak the language well and didn't know how to teach the spoken language.

The Japanese have an unquenchable thirst for English. English is a required subject in all schools. It's a well-known fact in Japan that any product will sell better if it has an English name.

Did I say English? I meant some word or phrase that Japanese people *think* is English. Since most people don't speak or understand English very well, some surprising words and phrases pop up. Many native-speaking English teachers in Japan call it "Japanglish" but my favorite term for it is "Manglish."

Japanese people in marketing and advertising use English words and phrases, but they often sound strange because of the context, a misspelling, wrong combinations, or appropriateness.

Advertisers in the US do the same thing creating new English-sounding words, but the Japanese try to do it without the advantage of knowing the language and culture well.

Take for example the non-dairy cream substitute for your coffee or tea. It's a powder, so they combined cream and powder and got *Creap*!

Context or appropriateness is an often-made mistake. How about a sports drink called *Sweat*? Yeah, there's some connection there, but... One of the other popular drinks is *Calpis* which of course is pronounced 'cow piss' since Japanese can't get the L sound quite right.

Then there's a fast-food lunch place called *Hot Boxes*. One of the McDonald's imitators over here is called *Moss Burger*.

Sometimes it's whole phrases that become part of a sales campaign. One is *For Beautiful Life*. This is a big conglomerate company with thousands of products, and they used this phrase for a lot of their products. I've seen ads for cosmetics, detergents, and even cars that end with *For Beautiful Life*.

Imitation is the sincerest form of flattery, so I wasn't surprised when I saw an apartment building with a sign by the door that said *For beautiful livingship*.

The old favorite that Japanese never seem to tire of is *Let's*. Of course, in correct English this would be followed by a verb–let's go, let's eat, let's get out of here, but not in Japan–*Let's Kiosk*, *Let's ANA* (Japanese airline), *Let's Pizza* (Japan's new national food), or *Let's Happy Beautiful Life!*

I discovered that the names of the cars Japanese companies sell in the US are different in Japan. The Nissan Sentra is called the *Bluebird*, and would an American buy a *Cedric*? (Toyota's Avalon).

Because the streets are so narrow, most people drive minicars, one is even named *Minica* (they can't say the "r" sound) and some of the names are a linguistic trip through hell. There's one called the *Guppy*, at least it looks like its name.

I almost cried the day I saw a car with a sensible name–the *City* car. Isn't that logical? Of course, then I realized that the Japanese are unable to make the "see" sound and always substitute the "she" sound, so it becomes the "shitty" car!

Now don't get the wrong idea, I like Japan a lot. I love the electrically heated toilet seats, and other really unique and useful products. it's just what they are doing to my native language that gets to me. Will it ever stop? Japanglish has become a never-ending source of entertainment for native English speakers living in Japan.

While living in Japan, I went to a lecture by a famous African writer, and he addressed the issue of linguistic imperialism. He told us how outsiders had come to Africa and forced people to learn English, Portuguese, or French, and, over several generations, those languages have become the most useful way for people from various tribal groups and outsiders to communicate.

The quote that stuck with me was, "English is our language now; don't try to tell us what's right and what's wrong in our own kind of English."

I guess I should just shut up!

Life in the USSR

My parents were typical representatives of what was called the "first-generation Soviet intelligentsia." They were the first in their families to get a university education.

However, the Soviet intelligentsia were not taught any "remnants of bourgeois false science." Instead, "The Theory and History of Scientific Communism" was beaten into their heads.

Luckily, not all could be brainwashed, definitely not my mother. Both her parents hated the Soviet system. Her mother, my grandmother Lydia, came from a wealthy and reputable family of Russian merchants.

After the Revolution of 1917, in accordance with "the People's Rule", the family lost everything they had. My grandfather was sent to Siberia for five years, and Grandmother tried to make ends meet.

From childhood, my mother heard nothing but bitter criticism of the Soviet system from her family. As the daughter of a bourgeois family, she was not allowed to finish high school and was sent to a vocational program. Only years later was she able to finish high school with honors and enter the Moscow Law Institute.

My father's life, on the other hand, could serve as a perfect example of the Soviet success story. He was the tenth child in a poor Jewish family who lived in a small Belorussian village.

When my father was a small child, he fell and hurt his back. With ten kids and no money, his parents could not give him any medical attention. However, when the boy started growing a hump at the age of seven, the family finally took him to the nearest doctor, but it was too late to reverse the problem.

My father was doomed to stay a hunchback for the rest of his life. Due to this misfortune, however, he benefited in ways that his siblings did not. He was not drafted into the army during World War II. So, he was not killed by the Nazis like his brothers and other Jews in the village were.

He had been sent to St. Petersburg to study because, with his disability, he was no good as a farm worker. As a result, he was the only one in the family to get a university degree. He never complained about his disability; on the contrary, he considered himself a very lucky man. My dad firmly believed in the Soviet system.

Because of the German invasion in WW II, the candy factory where my father worked was moved from Moscow to the capital of Kazakhstan.

My mother ended up in the same city because the Moscow Law Institute had also been moved there. At that time, my mother was married and had a three-year-old daughter. Mother also brought her parents with her, but her husband had to stay in Moscow for work.

My parents met in 1941 when my mother found a job in the accounting department of the candy factory. She became the only provider for the family of four. With her ration card and the meager pension of my grandparents, they were able to survive.

When the war was over and they both returned to Moscow, it turned out that my mother's husband had started another family.

My parents moved in together and just before my birth, they got married. My father was happy to have a woman he adored, and my mother valued his character, and the stability that finally came back into her life.

I don't recollect any fights or arguments between my parents except for one topic that inevitably turned my otherwise reasonable and quiet parents into bitter and angry opponents. It was, of course, politics.

"Nina, don't say that in front of the child!" I can still hear my dad's pleading whisper following one of my mother's sarcastic remarks as they watched the news on TV.

"Let her know the truth about this lousy regime!" my mom would hiss. They couldn't speak loudly because the neighbors might hear. Like most Moscow families, we were living in a communal apartment, sharing the kitchen and the bathroom with two other families.

Since my parents' heated arguments for and against the Soviet regime pervaded my childhood, teen, and college years, their shared, intense hatred of Stalin surprised me.

Each February elections to the Supreme Soviet were held. All Soviet citizens had to vote for "dear, beloved Comrade Stalin" because there were no other candidates. Avoiding this sacred responsibility was not an option, unless of course, you wanted to be prosecuted by the government.

As my parents were about to leave the house to go vote, my mother felt the first contractions. She was not due for another two weeks. My father called a taxi, and they went to the nearest clinic. The chief nurse started filling out the required forms.

Suddenly she frowned and said, "I can't admit you because I don't see the voting stamp on your papers." My father explained that they had intended to vote but had to rush to the clinic.

The nurse said, "I can't break the rules. Everybody who can't vote today was supposed to render an early vote, but you don't have that stamp either".

He explained that his wife's contractions had started early, but all arguments were useless in the face of the Soviet system.

Father asked for the physician in charge. The doctor came, but he couldn't help them either. "Admitting your wife, comrade, will cost us our jobs, if not worse!" he said. Father rushed out of the building and found another taxi.

My parents hurried to another hospital ten minutes away, and there, father immediately asked for the doctor on duty.

While they were waiting, my mother's water broke. In pain, she lay down on the floor in the hallway. It was clear that she could not be moved anywhere. The doctor came quickly.

This doctor proved to be more sympathetic and came up with a practical solution. "There is only one thing you can do, comrade", he said. "Go to the central voting office downtown and beg them to lend you a ballot box."

He wrote a note, and my father signed a paper which said that the hospital would admit my mother for labor "provided that she will submit her vote within 24 hours."

Mother was admitted, and dad rushed out. He returned to the hospital in the wee hours of the morning, exhausted and humiliated. He had had to plead, beg, and sign many papers. He had finally managed to get the box.

My mother marked the only square on the ballot with a trembling hand. As I was making my way into the world, my father was on his way back to return the ballot box.

I was born on Sunday morning, February 22, 1953, around 10 a.m. Shortly after, an elated baritone voice on the radio delivered the happy news: Comrade Stalin and the People's Deputies were elected by a 100% vote!

Just two weeks later, on the 5th of March, the same deep velvety baritone, but grief stricken this time, announced that the Father of All Soviet People had died. My parents were quite happy about this but had to keep quiet while celebrating the birth of a daughter into a new age in the USSR.

We all know how that 'new age' turned out which is why I now live in the United States.

Unusual and strange

I'm sharing these odd tales to honor the
trust their authors showed in sharing
them with me

The Butterfly

When I started out to my car getting ready to go to work, a beautiful, large butterfly greeted me on the front steps. It circled in front of me a few times. For some reason, I thought about my sweet friend who had died recently, and I felt a familiar sadness.

Strangely, the atmosphere seemed to change. Time seemed to slow down. I was in a state of being–I was only in the present moment–watching the butterfly fly so close to me.

For some reason, I reached out my hand and it landed on my palm. I contained my excitement the best I could for fear it would fly away. My beautiful butterfly friend lifted off and circled me again.

I thought about needing to get to work, but for some reason, instead I laid down on my back in the sweet-smelling grass with my knees up. I reached my arms and hands up to the sky.

The beautiful visitor landed on my palm again and I blurted out, "Holy shit, Peg, Is this you?!" A voice inside my mind asked, *Is this possible?*

The butterfly ascended and circled around me one more time. My eyes started to tear up as time stopped and a still peace enveloped me and the entire yard. It seemed that there was nothing outside this glorious, extraordinary bubble.

Then my visitor came back down and landed on my knee. "My God, you are so beautiful. This is amazing. Thank you", I whispered.

Still on my knee, its wings dropped. I didn't move because I felt so calm, savoring this precious experience. I waited while looking at all its details: colors, design, and form–so intricate, so perfect.

Tears began to leak from my eyes when I realized it had died…
on my knee…on me. *No! Why?!*

After a while, I laid my sweet visitor on the grass in a lovely
corner of my yard. The time clock had started up again. I drove
to work in a kind of trance. I don't remember much about getting
through that day.

Obviously, I have never forgotten this strange and wondrous
event that I experienced over 30 years ago and surely, I never will.

Some people say it was my friend letting me know she still lives
in peace and for me not to grieve–that death is only a transition.

I don't know what I believe. All I know is that something
significant happened that morning which mattered enough to
change me.

Something of a spiritual nature happened to me all those
years ago, unexpected and mind altering, and it propelled me to
seek spiritual knowledge even to this day.

I looked up the spiritual meaning of the butterfly. It means
transformation.

My Strange Dream

This contributor wrote, "This is an odd dream which has haunted me for a long time."

I walked into his room as he was listlessly looking alternately at the book on his desk and out the window. He looked up surprised but not unhappy to have a distraction.

With a smile, he asked me what he could do for me. He didn't recognize me. I told him that I was here to help him with some of his problems.

He gave me a quizzical look but motioned for me to sit down on the bed. I shook my head and motioned for him to stand up. He gave me a curious look but pushed back his chair and stood.

I held out my arms indicating that I wanted to hug him. He hesitated, looked over my shoulder out the open door, and then moved toward me.

He wrapped his arms around me in a light embrace. I radiated my unconditional love for him, and I heard him catch his breath as he felt it.

I simply said, "I am always here for you, and you are loved for exactly who you are." He grasped me tighter and let out one short sob.

He backed away then and really looked at me. Our eyes locked, and we gazed at each other for a few endless seconds, and then he knew that I was him.

I was the man he would become in the future reaching across time and space to let him know who he truly was, and who he would be someday.

True to form, he immediately wanted answers for all the things churning in his mind. I explained that all those experiences he regretted and thought he was responsible for were really growth exercises, and that it always takes 'two to tango.'

I tried to convince him that he shouldn't take responsibility for things that were beyond his power to influence. "Have no fear and no guilt," I told him.

I told him that everything would turn out all right as long as he listened to his intuition and acted consciously.

I knew that he understood at some deep level that I was telling him the truth, but at that time in his life he was not completely ready to accept and trust what I told him. He just nodded his head and smiled that teenage 'well, if you say so' kind of smile.

Empathy

I have always been sensitive to my surroundings. Most people feel something similar and react to people and places, but with me it is sometimes intense. I was in college before I found out there is a word for my condition–I'm an empath.

When I was young, it was both a gift and a curse. I understood on a deep level what people wanted from me, and I could bask in their happiness and contentment when I pleased them.

However, it was torture when those around me felt fear, pain, or sadness. I hated hospitals and funerals. My folks thought I was just acting up, but I felt these feelings deeply as if they were happening to me.

One time, my folks made me go with them to the hospital to visit one of Mom's friends who had just had a baby. While walking down the hall, I saw the name of a friend on one of the doors. I was shocked that someone my age would be in the hospital, so I went in the room.

It turned out that a distant relative, Gene, had taken his dad's Colt pistol and gone out behind the barn to practice his quick draw. These were the days when there were lots of cowboy shows on the TV.

The pistol went off when he tried to get it out of his pocket. The bullet hit a rock near his foot, ricocheted off the rock, bounced backwards where it ricocheted again after hitting the steel frame of the barn door, and finally lodged in his right buttock. He was happy to have a visitor, but he told me that he didn't want me to tell anyone what had happened. The problem was that when he told me about getting shot in the butt, I felt it. I walked with a limp for hours after that visit, and for several years after my butt cheek would hurt anytime I remembered the story.

I met a psychology professor in college who told me that I could probably control the depth of these feelings if I worked on it. He helped me experiment with several approaches, and some of them really did help. I can now feel when negativity is approaching, and I can make excuses or make an exit. At times, I feel as if I'm standing off watching myself. I see, hear, and understand, but I'm not empathizing. Of course, if it is a friend or family member, I can't control it; I still feel deeply for them.

This ability also helps me to decide quickly whether I need to spend time and energy on new people. I get a positive or negative vibe from people and usually don't waste time on those I don't want or need in my life. However, it is awkward when that person is important in the life of someone I care for. I can't very well tell someone not to marry that person when they think they are in love.

The most interesting and usually positive experience is music. Sometimes I can feel the joy that the composer or performer felt when that song was created or performed. Listening to Mozart is a pure joy. Bach was more complicated as there are happy and sad parts in most of his music. Some songs feel like resigned melancholy looking back at a sad event. Some songs make me want to dance and others make me sigh.

Art also gives me deep impressions from the artist and time the piece was created. When I went to the Louvre in Paris, I was almost overcome with the onslaught of feelings. I literally ran from all of Van Gough's paintings. I now prefer smaller galleries.

TV is a different experience for me. Most of it leaves me flat as it is not reality, but documentaries are another story. They are the real thing with real people and sometimes they feel really heavy as I live through the story with them.

Sometimes this ability takes a lot out of me. I don't feel it at the time as I am caught up in the feelings of others and the joining of their emotions to mine. After the experience is over, I'm exhausted, but I have to think of it as a gift.

This gift has made me better at my job. I'm a teacher. It is great to share the joy the young have for life, and the optimism that I feel from most of my students. I can use my gift to answer their needs–not only academically, but also emotionally. I use my knowledge and experience to try to prepare them for some of the mistakes I know they are going to make as they go through life no matter what I or other adults warn them about.

Being an empath has had both positive and negative effects on my life. But I have no choice, so I try to use my gift to help others and not let it trap me in the dark side.

The Path Along the Creek

The path along the creek was always my special place. There is a beautiful, small meadow near the creek where there is a log to sit on and enjoy the babbling brook, the dappled sunshine, and the rustle of the aspen leaves as the breeze blows.

I sat for a while enjoying the environment, and then got up and walked along the path. I crossed over the creek on the fallen tree.

Something made me look back, and suddenly I remembered sitting with a friend on that special log.

I remembered I was crying after my love had left me, and my soul sister was trying to empathize and comfort me. She tried to explain that the world would go on although she knew that, at that moment, there was no consolation.

I had always known that we were linked by karma. He came into my life to teach me how to love more completely, and my purpose in the relationship was to nudge him onto a higher spiritual path, so that he could, in turn, positively influence others.

I shook my head; that was so long ago. Why was that memory haunting me now? I turned and followed the path along the creek. I hadn't been here for quite a while, so I was surprised by some changes that blocked the path ahead.

The voice in my head said, "What do you see?"

"Trees have fallen and blocked the path. It seems dark and dangerous ahead."

"Listen to your feelings. Trust your perceptions; stay on the right path" the voice whispered.

I looked around and noticed that there was a mossy area on the opposite bank. I thought I could probably jump over the creek although the distance between the banks had widened.

"Life is full of challenges; don't let yourself get too comfortable and stagnate," the voice intoned.

I measured the distance with my eyes, backed up to get up some speed, and went for it. The bank on my side gave way as I launched myself, but I made it far enough to land with most of my body on the mossy shoulder. One shoe got a little wet, but I quickly scrambled up and sat on a rock to catch my breath.

After a quick look back across the creek, I went on down the path on the sunnier side of the creek. As I came around a small curve, the sun lit up a tree ahead with a golden glow.

As I got nearer, I recognized the tree. It was the tree where we had left some of our musical father's ashes.

I found a place to sit and thought of all the things he had taught me. What a magical man he had been.

I was nearing the end of the trail when the remains of the ancient medicine wheel came into view. It was not as I remembered it.

Earlier in my life, it had been alive with stones of various colors, crystals, shells, rattles, skins, drums, and the most amazing variety of people of all ages and types.

I remembered the day I was asked by my sister to sit with her in the center and help with some of the rituals. It was a great honor, and only one of many she has given me over the years.

Now the medicine wheel seemed empty. So much was missing, the sawn log seats, the stones, the colorful paraphernalia. The sacred fires had long since gone cold.

I found a comfortable place and sat down to meditate. Slowly, I became aware of shadows floating into the ancient circle from the forest.

I realized that in fact, the wheel was more sacred now than before. All the unnecessary paraphernalia and the sometimes meaningless rituals were gone. Only the true spirit of the place remained, and the universe loved the place as it was now.

As I came out of meditation, the voice of my higher self said, "Take heart–never fear! You have never failed although you sometimes think you have. Trust yourself and stay on the right course. Walk on, and enjoy the journey, whatever it brings"

The blessing that was given by the sun's glow on the mountain side, the creek, and the trees moved my heart, and I was filled with a sense of uplifting joy.

Believe It or Not

I have been interested in spiritual beliefs since I was a boy. My attitude has been more scientific and objective even though such beliefs are mostly personal and subjective. I try to understand as deeply as I can, but I withhold judgment – neither believing nor disbelieving.

In my view, all things are possible, but none are proven. However, I had an experience in Spain which shook my attitude and approach.

I was standing in line waiting for the ticket office of a famous museum to open along with other tourists from all over the world. I felt something rubbing against my lower leg and turned to look. It was a small boy, maybe six or seven years old.

His mother, who was talking to his father, noticed, and said something to him in German. I know some German, so I knew that she had called him by name – Felix, but I didn't understand some of the vocabulary that she used.

I assumed she told him to leave me alone because he said to her in perfect English, "But I know him." She leaned down and picked him up. Then he turned to me and when we were face to face, he said again, "I know you."

As a sort of joke, I said, "And I know you, Felix." At that moment, something I will never be able to explain passed between us. His blue eyes were locked on mine, and we both began to tear up. He reached out for me and I took him in my arms. He snuggled up and laid his head on my shoulder.

His mother looked at me closely, and then with a small shake of her head said, "You must be one of the group that came before. You don't know how thankful I am to not have to excuse and explain Felix's words and actions. Most people don't know about or believe in reincarnation."

Still at a loss for words from the power of this odd experience, I just muttered, "Umm" and turned my attention back to Felix holding on so tightly. Taking a deep breath, I asked, "Has he done this often?"

"No, of course not. Only one other time. It didn't turn out so well." She hesitated and then went on, "Felix is not the name we gave him when he was born. He told us his name was Felix when he was three. That was when we first became aware that he was special."

"How is he able to speak English so well?" I asked.

"My husband and I both work for international companies and use a lot of English at home, and of course he has a lot of music and DVDs in English," she replied. "But we suspect there is more to it than that. He speaks better than we do," she laughed.

The suspicious part of my mind floated a thought that this might be an elaborate scam of some kind, but the rest of my mind immediately squashed that idea due to the depth and purity of the feelings that accompanied this experience.

Then Felix's father stepped up and said, "The ticket booth is opening."

Felix's mother moved to take Felix back into her arms, but he held on a little longer and said, "You came too early this time, Lucas. Next time wait for me. I love you." Then he kissed me and let go and turned toward his mother.

My mind was spinning like a tornado as I stumbled to the window and bought my ticket. I assumed I would get to talk to Felix more inside and ask some of the many questions swirling through my mind like why he called me Lucas, but when I turned around, the family was walking away.

I heard Felix's father say, "I thought you wanted to see this museum."

Felix smiled up at him and said, "I saw what I came here for," and happily skipped down the street not looking back.

Reincarnation

Do I believe in reincarnation? I don't know, but I do know that I am more comfortable in some places in the world than others. The first time I was in Japan, I felt a strange familiarity with the place, the culture, and the people.

Did I live there before? I have had that same strange "I'm home" feeling in Portugal and Southern France. One of my friends refers to these places as our 'karmic homes.' There is no logical reason why I should feel so connected to these foreign places, but the feeling is overwhelming when it comes.

I grew up a farm boy in the Midwest. Going to another state was considered a big trip even though it was only an hour away. Since then, I have traveled to many countries, but in most places, I'm just a tourist like everyone else.

Another strange experience that might be related to this concerns books. When I read certain books about a time or a place or a culture, I experience the environment of the story completely. I instinctively know how things smell or sound, or what the weather is like in that place.

I have occasionally recommended books to friends telling them how wonderful the writer and story are, and then I am surprised when they don't enjoy the book as much as I did.

One time a friend actually went through a book with me to figure out why I had liked it, and when I told him how the setting looked and smelled and about the weather in that part of the world, he said, "But none of that is in this book. How do you know that? It's not written down that way."

I occasionally meet people for the first time and feel that I recognize them or have known them before. They seem like old familiar friends even though we have just met. Sometimes it seems like we can read each other's minds after only a few minutes together. Some call that personal resonance.

Do I believe in reincarnation? Well, I don't dismiss the idea, but I'm still not sure. Although these experiences are very real to me, I still have to live my life everyday whether this is one life of many, or the only one I will ever have. I do know that my attitude makes me feel more comfortable when making any decision.

Recognizing My Inner Child

I was sitting in meditation on a flat rock near the lake. It was one of my favorite places to meditate with the soft sounds of the water and gentle shade from the tall trees all around.

I heard someone coming down the path – the crack of a broken stick, a sniffle, a sigh. I opened my eyes as a young, blond child came out of the bushes across from me.

As I looked at him, he looked back at me with intelligent eyes. Suddenly, I was able to see myself, both as an innocent child and as an adult.

I smiled at him and saw the decision to trust me cross his face clearly. I motioned for him to come closer.

He came and stood in front of me. We didn't speak. Tears started leaking from the corners of his eyes. "Why don't they like me?" he said.

I opened my arms and folded him onto my lap, kissing his head and saying, "It will be all right. That other stuff doesn't matter now. You're safe here."

My own tears started flowing as I remembered all the little hurts of childhood. "They are afraid of you because you're different, but that doesn't matter. When you grow older, it will be your secret power. Just remember that you are special, and it won't hurt so much."

He twisted on my lap to look me in the face. "Really," he asked.

"Yes, really," I answered.

He turned and leaned back against my chest and sighed. We listened to the wind in the leaves and the sound of the waves.

Military Memories

Sometimes the duties of citizenship are
life-changing

The Unsolved Mystery of a WW I Pilot

On November 3rd, 1918, an armistice between Italy and Austria was signed to go into effect 24 hours later. On the day after the armistice was signed, my uncle, Flight Commander Franz Rudorfer, 21 years old, flew over the Italian lines by mistake and was shot at by a platoon of Italian soldiers. One bullet penetrated though the bottom of his fighter plane.

Franz was not able to land his plane. He crashed and was found hunched over the controls lifeless. The Italians gave him a military burial, and eventually sent an account of the event, his belongings as well as the plane's insignia back over the Austrian lines.

Exactly a week later in the evening, his parents and younger siblings were sitting at the dinner table when suddenly his stand-up picture fell over on its face. In the hushed silence my great-aunt said, "Franzi is dead", whereupon my great-uncle said, "Hush, woman, he is not dead. The war is over!"

The above is recorded in our family lore, but is it true? Franz Rudorfer was supposedly buried in a cemetery near Turin reserved for Austrian war casualties. Two years later his parents visited that cemetery, intending to affect a transfer of his body to the family crypt in Vienna, but there was no trace of his grave and no records were ever found.

A year after their Turin visit, in 1921, a newspaper clipping was found in the prayer book of a departed lady in the town of Meran, formerly part of Austria, and after the war, a part of Italy.

The news article read, "Death fall of a former Austrian Flyer. One of the most famous and well-known fighter pilots of the former Austrian army, Major Franz Rudorfer, former Commander of Fighter Squadron # 51, fell out of his plane to his death on Nov. 13, over Turin, and was killed instantly. His plane crashed nearby, causing no damage to people or property."

"The accident is made especially sad by the fact that Major Rudorfer had just been chosen to assume a leading role in the newly created International Postal Air Service and had recently married. No further details are known."

My uncle's family was quite upset by this information because it was so different from what they thought that they knew about what had happened to Uncle Franz.

This new information about Franz Rudorfer's death and marriage remained a mystery to his family. The search for information was even more obscured by the ascendancy of Benito Mussolini in Italy and WW II. The Austrian government had no record of him having been chosen to lead the Postal Air Service. No documented evidence of where he was buried, or any other mention of Franz's marriage ever came to light.

His parents spent their meager fortune trying to establish what had really happened. Did their son survive his supposed battle-death in 1918 and then die a married man in an unverifiable accident in 1921?

Eventually the family held a ceremonial burial at the crypt in Vienna where the names of the men in the family who died in war are chiseled into the headstone, now including my Uncle Franz Rudolfer.

The Memories are Always There

He was always there just inside the front door of Grandma's house. I knew it. I felt it. After closing the heavy door with the gold star decal affixed to the glass, I instinctively paused a moment in the cool, dim light at the foot of the stairs.

I never knew my uncle, but he was there in spirit on the hall table. A bronze-framed, hand-tinted photograph of Grandma and Grandpa's wedding was flanked by a delicate porcelain figurine. It depicted a seated mother with a young boy and girl at her knee.

It was special because it had been given to Grandma by her two children, my mother and her younger brother, on Mother's Day just before he joined the Navy. There was also an amber bud vase which often held a sprig of fern or a single white carnation.

My uncle died in an air attack while serving in the South Pacific in WW II. As was the tradition then, he was buried at sea.

Every year, our family attended the Memorial Day service in the municipal park in our small town. At the end of the program, Grandma received a single white carnation from the American Legion Commander to acknowledge that she was a Gold Star mother, a mother whose son had made the ultimate sacrifice for his country.

Single white carnations, a bugler playing taps, and the singing of God Bless America still bring tears to my eyes even today, as those things did then.

All those people getting up on the stage and talking, talking, talking often made me impatient. If I was squirming on a wooden folding chair next to the War Memorial fountain, I would find my hand or shoulder being squeezed to tell me to settle down. They squeezed because they were afraid their voices would crack with emotion if they tried to speak.

Even though I was young, I could see the private pain hidden behind tear-stained eyes in all the adults who were there for the yearly ceremony. They had all lost someone dear to them. I could feel their grief.

Grandma frequently lamented that there was no grave, no marker for my uncle. Finally, with the American Legion's help, Grandpa got a bronze plaque to honor him. My grandparents placed it in the middle of the double plot they had reserved for their own graves.

What I Learned in the USMC

I've always felt like a 'lucky' person, if that is what being in the right place at the right time means. My grandma always called it being blessed. I have learned that if you remain open and neutral, life will naturally point you in the right direction.

When people ask me why I did a certain thing, if I don't know the answer, I know it is because I was open at that time to whatever was coming next in my life. I didn't actively choose, so maybe Grandma was right, and it was some sort of divine nudging.

For instance, I don't know why I joined the Marine Corps. It seemed very unlikely to everyone who knew me, and I couldn't say why I did it; but now, with hindsight, I can see that it was a very important event in the overall flow of my life.

In the Marine Corps, I learned that I was above average physically, that I understood discipline better than most, that my ability to please others was a valuable skill; and I learned how to keep my mouth shut.

Being a Marine provided me with experiences I couldn't have gotten anywhere else, the financial resources to finish my college degree, some friends I have kept in touch with through the years, the experience of living and working in another country, and a certain status in American society as a veteran.

In Vietnam, I learned that some people have no willpower and that for them drugs were a one-way street. It was easy to see that some people can justify any act, no matter how despicable by using God or country.

I also learned that some people cannot tell the difference between the symbols for things, and what they stand for like the flag. I saw that many people do not realize when their actions and ideas actually contradict their actions and ideas at other times.

I saw how some people are imprinted for life by family, region, religion, or experience, and that some people are not affected by those same factors as much and are open to change.

I began my long avocation as a people watcher when I was a Marine. I especially like to watch the various ways the males of our species present themselves to the world. There are thousands of variations, none of which is the one true definition of a man.

I suppose I could go on and on but suffice it to say that although I don't know why I became a Marine, I know that I was in the right place at the right time when I began that journey, and I don't regret any of it.

Brothers in War

My grandparents had six children, five boys born like clock-work in 1892, '94, '96, '98, and 1900. This is a war story about the brothers.

When Archduke Maximilian of the Austro-Hungarian Empire was assassinated in Sarajevo in 1914, the "War to End all Wars" soon began. My grandparents' first three sons gave their lives for "Gott, Kaiser, und Vaterland"–for God, Emperor, and Fatherland– at the Russian front between 1914 and 1916.

During that time, the fourth born, Emmerich, had begun a carpentry apprenticeship, and earned a master's certificate. Little did he know that this would save his life 40 years later. Emmerich was by all accounts always a polite and helpful young man, quiet and somewhat shy. He and his younger brother were exempt from military service by the fact that his parents had lost three sons already. Then surprisingly, Emerich suddenly volunteered for the Army.

In tears, my grandmother begged him not to go. My grand-father was more stoic and supposedly just said, "Son, stay alive for us!" Emmerich went off and was assigned to the Italian front after basic training in Vienna. After a rather uneventful year of stationary warfare, his commander ordered an all-out attack on the Italian lines. Emmerich was hit in the chest by a stray bullet in December 1917.

Luckily, this ended the war for him. Emmerich spent months in a hospital to regain his full health again. It seems doubtful that he fully recovered from the mental shock of being shot because of what happened two months later.

No sooner had WW I ended than Emmerich volunteered for the Hungarian Army, which was fighting the troublemaking Romanians. The Hungarians got their butts kicked, and my uncle escaped with only the loss of half of his left ear, which was hit by shrapnel. Back to Vienna he went and started working on several major construction projects in Austria.

That peaceful interlude lasted until 1936, when Emmerich joined the International Brigades fighting against Franco in Spain. He participated in seven major battles and countless smaller encounters mostly with German fighter planes. Hitler and the Nazis were testing their newest planes by aiding Franco in the Spanish Civil War. Emmerich later told the family that his battery had certifiably downed 15 Nazi planes. He was hit in the left foot by a machine gun bullet, severing two of his toes.

At the end of that ill-fated war many Austrian and German members of the International Brigades tried to escape over the border into France rather than fall into Franco's hands. However, they were held in France, interned there for a year, and eventually handed over to the Germans after France surrendered to the Nazis in 1940.

The Germans promptly forced the over 3,000 Germans and Austrians into their troops, and Emmerich found himself a part of the troops in the infamous "Siege of Leningrad" from 1941 to 1943. He saw little action, but he lost two fingers on his right hand due to frostbite.

In 1943, a German Officer lined up the soldiers, and asked, "Who among you has construction experience, and speaks French?" Quickly Emmerich stepped forward and was promptly transferred to France. There he began supervising the building of a segment of the German defensive fortifications against the anticipated Allied invasion.

History now tells us that the problem was that the heaviest and strongest defenses were built around Calais. None of the

Nazi strategists had considered an Allied landing attempt any-where else but the shortest distance from England.

In June of 1944, Emmerich was transferred to Normandy where, on the third day of the allied invasion, he was buried by a col-lapsing tunnel hit by allied bombardment and had a skull injury.

He and the other wounded were taken to a convent, where one of the French lay-sisters, Francine, helped nurse him back to health. Three years after the war, nurse Francine visited Emmerich in Vienna, and they married shortly thereafter. It must have been true love, because who would marry a meek little fellow with a huge scar in his chest, having two toes, two fingers and half an ear missing, and large, red scar running over his head?

That ended my uncle's military exploits, and in his old age he became an unending source of fascinating stories about his narrow escapes. His modest little home across the Danube was filled with love and compassion.

When Aunt Francine passed away in 1984, he visited her grave every day, talking to her as if she were sitting next to him, which he knew she surely was even though he couldn't see her. He lived to be 89 years old.   Those wars didn't get my Uncle Emmerich.

War Changes People

When I arrived in Da Nang, Vietnam, in 1970, I was new to the place and the odd man out. Luckily, there was one guy there at the Marine air base that I had been stationed with in Southern California. We had been friends for several years, and our wives were good friends, too. John took me under his wing and showed me the ropes.

I have noticed that when men find themselves in a large group of isolated males, they immediately form tribes. I found that the Marines in my squadron had a number of tribes, and new guys were sort of vetted, recruited, and then adopted into one of the tribes. I had an almost immediate acceptance into the tribe my buddy John belonged to.

It was only later that I found out that my particular group had quite a reputation. They had an unusual competition going on. They constantly tried to "out weird" each other.

Now if this sounds strange, stress was high at that time as the giant ammo dump near the base had just blown up when a missile hit it, and missiles flew over the camp almost every evening although they rarely hit anything. Of course, Marines couldn't talk about their fears, so there was a lot of acting up to compensate and blow off steam.

Every evening this group gathered together to talk, laugh, drink beer, and smoke marijuana. The Vietnamese pot was especially potent. Maybe it was natural that things got a little weird, but they turned it into a competition.

It was very hot in Vietnam, so every day as soon as we got back from dinner, we showered, put on clean boxers and t-shirts and went to our evening get-together to cool off. One evening when we were sitting around listening to music and getting high, one of the guys slapped a large cockroach off a buddy's back. Immediately, someone in the group yelled, "Eat it!

The guy leaned back and said, "I prefer my roaches roasted," making a joke as pot cigarettes were often called roaches.

Right away, three or four people flicked open their Zippo lighters. Then someone stabbed the dead cockroach with a chopstick and proceeded to roast the thing.

After a couple of deep drags of marijuana, that guy reached over and ate the thing! That night he won the competition and was crowned the king of weird for the evening.

Pot was also part of the initiation into our tribe, so of course after a week or so, it was my turn. Since John was my sponsor, it was up to him to 'smoke me in.'

John turned a roach around in his mouth, clutching the wet end in his front teeth. The burning end was then inside his mouth which freaked me out.

Then I was instructed to cup my hands around his nose and mouth and inhale as he blew smoke out of his nose. This went on for two or three breaths, or when John felt the roach getting too hot in the back of his mouth. It made me higher than I liked to be.

It was a very intimate kind of thing to do, but I observed several rather intimate interactions over the year that I was in Vietnam. I think it's something that happens in the military when you are far from home and family and fear for your safety and your life. Your group of friends really are like your brothers.

There were two or three main leaders of the weirdness in the group, and they were always trying to come up with crazy stuff to better their rivals. All the leaders had their buddies who often helped them with their schemes. I soon realized that my buddy John was one of the kingpins, and that he expected me to become his helper.

We also drank lots of beer at our nightly gatherings. Sometimes the combination of booze and pot would sneak up on some of the guys, and when that happened, we would carry them off unconscious to their sleeping area.

One evening, one of the guys got up to go to the latrine to relieve himself. One of the leaders stopped the guy and dared him to piss in his beer. Several in the group encouraged him to do it, but he said he didn't think he could do it in front of an audience.

My buddy John got up and coolly whipped out his dick, and not only pissed in his beer, but when the bottle was full, he pissed all over the guy! Wow! What an uproar ensued as both the guy who was pissed on and John wanted to claim the evening's weirdness crown.

John then told the group that he would let anyone piss on him. He looked at me, but I shook my head. The original guy who had been pissed on then stood up and pissed all over John. In the end, they ended up hugging and laughing and taking off their smelly t-shirts and boxers and staggering off to the showers.

As time went on and I was never called on to be personally involved in any of the weirdness, I thought I was safe. That was a big mistake. My time was coming.

One evening when we got back to our living area, we found that something had happened to the water supply, so we couldn't take our usual evening showers.

At the evening get together, people were complaining about being hot and sweaty and smelly. John gave me a long look, then got out a small pan that one of the guys used to make tea. He filled it with beer and started up the small grill.

People were looking at him curiously, but he was just stirring the pan and singing along to a song on the stereo. Finally, he stood up and came over to me. "Stand up," he said. I was confused about what he was up to, but he was my buddy, so I stood up.

Immediately, he pulled down my USMC issued khaki-green boxers. I grabbed and covered my privates, and he directed me to step out of my shorts.

He then put my sweaty skivvies into the beer bubbling in the pan. He sat back down and continued stirring. Now everyone was wondering what he was up to. The anticipation was growing. I sat back down feeling a little vulnerable since I was naked from the waist down.

We all knew that it was one of John's last nights with us as he had received his orders to go back stateside the next week. Usually, when someone got their orders to go back to the US, they were happy and liked to rub it in.

He had been sort of quiet for the last week, and I thought that maybe he was going to miss our little crazy get-togethers and probably his status in our tribe. I knew that I was going to miss him for sure.

John then broke out a small bottle of brandy and added it to the pan of liquid. "Ok, tea's on!" he said and started pouring the liquid out of the pan into a cup. It was steaming, so he said, "I've got to cool it," and went to the small refrigerator and got out some ice.

Everyone was staring at him. Was he actually going to drink tea made from beer and my sweaty underwear? I figured that he would as he was a science guy and would know that the alcohol in the beer and brandy and the boiling temperature would kill off any germs.

I thought that this was a chance to show my support as his buddy. I just sort of smiled and said, "I'd like a cup."

He smiled from ear to ear and filled another cup. By that time of the evening, people were well into their third or fourth beer and had been puffing on several roaches, so they were all very mellow. Everyone was waiting to see if we would go through with it.

Finally, John picked up the first cup and tasted it. "Ah, just right," he pronounced.

I had forgotten my embarrassment about being naked and got up to get my cup. When I bent over to pick up the cup, one of the other guys slipped out of his seat, slid across the floor, and kissed my ass!

I was frozen for a moment. Everyone was stunned and silent waiting to see what would happen next. Then my buddy winked at me, so I turned around and said in a threatening voice, "If you ever do that again," I stopped, hesitated, and then in an imitation of Paul Lynde said, "I just might marry you."

The guys went nuts shrieking, screaming, and laughing!

John got to be the King of Weird one last time.

A Boyhood Dream

The air-raid sirens were howling again, their pitch rising and falling, telling us that soon Allied bombers would be flying over our heads. They were following the course of the Danube River to bomb our city, Vienna, and maybe going on to bomb Budapest as well.

It was the spring of 1944, and the frequency of air-raids in Vienna had increased tremendously. Most women with small children were being evacuated to the countryside, which was considered safer from bombings.

All school classes were cancelled. My mother was given the name and address of a family in a small town upriver from Vienna where we were to report. The very next day my younger brother and I carried our little rucksacks with a few items of clothing while our mom dragged a huge suitcase filled with basic necessities for the three of us. How long would we be gone? Nobody knew.

Early the next morning, a large group of mothers and children assembled near the city center. They were put on several German army trucks according to their destinations. This was all very exciting for us kids, but none of the women were smiling. Only much later did we understand what anxiety must have filled the hearts and minds of our mothers. Their husbands were fighting somewhere. Their homes might be damaged or destroyed, and people were being shipped off to unknown places, and an unknown future for them and their children.

Soon the dozens of trucks rumbled off in various directions. Our truck followed the road upriver along the Danube past ancient castles, fortresses, abbeys, and through tiny towns along the river. As the trucks reached their assigned destinations, families got off at towns along the way. Finally, we reached our assigned little town.

The truck stopped at the house where we were to be hosted. The Danube was rolling by just a hundred feet away.

A surly looking woman received us, and showed us to a tiny, dingy room at the back of the building. She was quite obviously not pleased about having to accommodate and feed us for an unknown period of time even though the hosts were being paid by the government.

The room had most likely been a storage area before we arrived. It was dusty and full of spider webs. It measured about twelve by fifteen feet. There were two cots piled on top of one another, a storage chest, a wood-burning oven, and a tiny table with three half-broken chairs. There was an outhouse in the back and an outside sink.

The woman came in our new room, and without a word, set down a pot of food and left. We devoured it like hungry little wolves as we had not eaten much since early morning. We had only had a slice of bread with margarine spread on it. Our mom began to clean up the room, setting the bad furniture to rights as best she could. She told us that we would probably spend quite some time here until the unforeseeable end of the war.

I can't remember much about the next several months, except those two or three times a week bomber squadrons flew over the Danube River on their way to Vienna. One event, however, stands out in my memory as if it had happened yesterday.

Another raid was in progress, and my brother and I were watching from a little sandbank a few feet from the Danube shore. German Anti-Aircraft guns were firing from the hills on both sides of the Danube as usual, but for the first time, they actually hit a plane, and we could clearly see several parachutes in the sky floating down a few kilometers away.

A little while later, we heard somebody yelling, *"Ami Flieger sind in der Stadt!"* (American flyers are in the town!) My brother and I ran along the tree-lined street leading to the center of town. There were several captured American airmen sitting in the beer garden with the local Austrian soldiers drinking beer while dozens of curious townspeople watched. The Americans were giving cigarettes to the soldiers.

My brother and I were staring in fascination. No one had ever seen one of those mythical creatures, an American airman! We had been told they were some sort of horrible monsters, but they looked just like us and seemed to be friendly.

One of the American POW airmen saw us two boys staring at them and said something to the German soldiers. Then he came down the steps toward us. As he stood before us, he reached into his pocket, and gave each of us something wrapped in paper. He then stuck one in his own mouth and said, "chewing gum", and made chewing motions with his mouth. We followed his example, and for the first time in our lives experienced that unique sensation, a part of the "American Dream" called chewing gum!

A few minutes later a German soldier on a motorcycle came by and yelled something to the officer. The officer quickly ordered the American POWs and his soldiers back on their truck, and in a moment, they were gone.

A little while later another truck rolled in with a group of black-uniformed soldiers. They stopped and asked the old innkeeper something. The man shook his head, pointed, and I could hear was the SS-officer shout, *"Scheisse, die Amis sind schon weg!"* (Shit, the Americans are gone already!) The POWs were indeed lucky, because the SS would most likely have executed them on the spot.

It was on this unforgettable day that I knew with absolute certainty that one day I wanted to be an American airman, fly above the clouds, and chew gum.

That never came to pass, but I have become an American citizen and have taught foreign languages in high school for more than 50 years.

CPSIA information can be obtained
at www.ICGtesting.com
Printed in the USA
LVHW111507131222
735135LV00004B/204